Celtic Wisdom and Wit:

a collection of Scottish Gaelic proverbs

translated into English, illustrated, and with notes on culture and language

Compiled and edited by

mìcheal mac an t-saoir

illustrations by

Tuigse Nic Fhuadain

Part of the series

Learning Gaelic through Reading

copyright 2024

published by

Seanchaidh

Cha dean duine dona ach a dhìcheall.

A poor fellow can do but his best.

Contents

𝕮𝖊𝖑𝖙𝖎𝖈 𝖂𝖎𝖘𝖉𝖔𝖒 𝖆𝖓𝖉 𝖂𝖎𝖙: 1

***Dùthaich -- Heritage* 4**

Remember! 5

Land of our ancestors 7

Against the rocks 10

To speak imperfectly 12

Language as a part of *dùthaich* 14

A people without a language 15

Use it or lose it 16

The hardships 18

All the water in the ocean 21

The sweetest music 23

Children of the Gael! 25

***Work and Success* 40**

Patience 47

Great things achieved ... 49

Working together 52

Sowing and reaping 54

Stick to what you're doing 56

Experience & practice 58

And not just any practice 60

***Values* 62**

What will last 63

Highland hospitality 65

Are you a man or a dog? 68

Don't be a dung-beetle 70

Generosity 72

A happy home 74

Beauty 75

The corrupting influence of having too much 81

A corrolary to this proverb 91

True riches 92

Wisdom 94

Imagination vs. reality 97

When you're down and out 99

Enjoy the good while it lasts 105

A small spark 108

He who accuses 110

Inevitability 113

Where the pigs are 115

The best sauce 118

In the shadows 120

Steal a little 122

The company you keep 126

Where you come from 128

Your greatest enemy 130

Necessity 132

What makes a table 134

The insight of a friend's eye 136

Quiet waters, and thin streams 138

A little piece for the beast. 140

Fate 143

Concealing evil 146

The impossible 149

Speaking of oars 151

Love, Gaelic style 155

Whether you want it or not 156

Doubt and love 159

Birds of a feather 163

The nature of love 165

Love of sailors 168

Of love, honey, and bees 170

Wit 173

Aren't you the lucky one! 176

Wise fools 177

Occupational hazards 179

The never-ending quest 181

A horse and water 185

On getting it 187

Life advice 192

Deeds not words 193

Life-long learning 195

Good advice, not always followed 197

Life changes 202

Talking sense to a fool 205

Gain and loss 207

Desperate times 209

Go with what you've got 212

Clean your own house 214

The hero's quest 220

Strength vs. cunning 221

Kindness as a heroic quality 223

Surviving by your wits 225

The fate of heroes 227

Goals 229

Principal Sources 231

a good place for us to start

An seanfhacal gu fada fìor, cha bhriagaichear e.

**The old saying long proved true shall never be belied
(that is, proved false).**

Perhaps the best place for us to start, this *seanfhacal* – "old word," or "old saying" -- about proverbs themselves asserts the enduring truth of ancient, time-tested folk wisdom. In a sense, time does to these adages what water does to stone: tests them, wears them smooth, polishes all the dirt and untruth from them, until they are left with no jagged edges, and they are hardened, rounded, and smoothed.

Old sayings don't live on in people's memories because someone has declared them important. They're remembered because each generation finds them to be true and applicable to daily life and experience.

We shouldn't make the mistake of thinking that being "true," they're all the work of Serious Seumas, a stern teacher in a black coat standing over naughty children with a switch in his hand, for sometimes the proverbs we find in this book are fun. (Which is part of the point too!); in here we find wisdom comingled with wit. Sometimes, they're funny; sometimes they're heartwarming; sometimes they remind us of what's important; sometimes, they advise us of the correct course; sometimes they warn us of dangers we might encounter along the way.

And always, the sayings in this book are little lights of wisdom and wit passed down to us from our ancestors, gleaming pinpricks of light that shine like stars in a clear night sky guiding us home as we stumble along an unlighted path on a dark night.

In addition, those who are perusing this selection for insight into Gaelic culture, keep in mind that the values and the observations revealed here lend great insight into Gaelic culture – Gaelic values, Gaelic society, and even Gaelic material culture -- by which is meant, the tools ancient Gaels used, the conditions of their lives, how they made their livelihoods, and the environment in which they lived. As a quick example of how it is so that a folk saying might reflect some aspect of material culture, we should consider that a people looks to its social, cultural, and physical environment for metaphors and examples to express its ideas. Just as American sayings reflect elements of American culture -- "rocket science," "behind the eightball," "hit it out of the ballpark," "touch base," or "jump on the bandwagon," none of which would make any sense outside of the American experience -- in these pages, you'll see many references to cattle, herding, rowing, and the like (but none to rockets or baseball) that are all aspects of life in the traditional Highlands, and all of which give us insight to what that life was like.

Dùthaich -- Heritage

(and so much more)

Remember!

Cuimhnich air na daoine bhon tàinig thu.

Remember those you came from.

What Alexander Nicolson, a collector of Gaelic proverbs calls "A very Highland sentiment," perhaps derived from the traditional adherence to the clan system. Somebody else commented in a slightly less complementary tone that *genealogy is the opiate of the Gael*.

In the United States, when we first meet somebody, we often ask, *what do you do?* as if one's occupation is a defining feature of a person. However, in Gaelic culture, it is often the family from which one comes that defines a person.

There's a Gaelic phrase that is very often uttered when people first meet: *Cò às a tha thu?* (or *sibh*, if the circumstances call for more formal discourse).

This is more often than not translated as "**Where** do you come from?" and indeed, nowadays, this is now it is conventionally understood, and there are some linguists who posit that the "*Cò*" is actually a contraction for *càite*, "where." But applying the principle of Ogham's razor – namely that the simplest answer is more likely than not the right answer – this question might be understood with the direct and simplest translation of the word *cò* – "**Who** are you from?"

Once, many years ago when I first started learning Gaelic in a classroom setting, we students were invited to introduce ourselves by discussing why we were learning Gaelic. I opened up by talking about where my grandmother had come from – Poolewe, a little village on the northwest coast of Scotland. This sparked the instructor's interest and several questions – but what seemed to drive her inquiries was not the *where* my grandmother had come from, but rather the *who* she and her people were as far back as I could trace them.

I got the feeling from this that in my discussing *who* I had come from allowed the Gaelic instructor to get a 'fix' on me and form an understanding – at least as far as she was concerned -- who **I** was.

Language Notes

cuimhnich – the imperative of the verb that translates as "remember." The imperative is formed from the root verb, that is, the word you see in the dictionary when you look it up. The Gaelic imperative does inflect differently when the speaker is "commanding" more than one person. The verb takes on the plural imperative form, which would be the root word +*aibh* or +*ibh*, so in this case, if I were telling a bunch of people to remember, I would say, *cuimhichibh*.

cuimhnich _air_ – In English, we remember something – that is, the 'something' we're remembering is the object of the verb. In Gaelic, we remember **on** something (*air*) – the 'something' is the object of the preposition.

Land of our ancestors

Is còir do dhuine dàimh a bhith aige ri dùthaich na h-Athraichean aige.

A Person ought to have an attachment to the land of his ancestors

Monolingual speakers often do not adequately understand that words in one language do not necessarily "mean" (or exactly mean) corresponding words in another language. I have encountered the frustration that some students of Gaelic have as they wrestle with the fact that a single word in Gaelic does not denote a corresponding and precisely equivalent word in English. We should understand that the dictionary equivalent is sometimes just an approximation that hits at a common understanding of the word, often not its limitations or its breadth and scope. An underlying issue might be what a teacher of mine referred to as the *polysemic* nature of Gaelic words (containing multiple meanings); it's quite common for Gaelic words to 'pack' multiple meanings, sometimes dependent upon context, and sometimes … well, just *because*.

Another Gaelic tutor of mine, a dear friend -- Donald Mcdonald of Montreal, Quebec (a native speaker from the Isle of Harris in Scotland) -- used to correct me when I used a Gaelic word inappropriately. He'd ask me what I meant, and when I told him, he'd say, "Ach chan eil sinn ga chleachdadh mar sin" – *but we don't use it like that.*

Dùthaich is one such word, for which there is not really an adequate equivalent in English. Here, the translator gives "land," but in Gaelic the word *dùthaich* means so much more, its implications go so much deeper, although the word can refer to the English words for land, landscape, country, or countryside, these English words do not do justice to the full extent of meaning packed into *dùthaich*. There is a sense of the word in which place (the physical landscape) becomes co-extensive and intermingled with personal memories, ancestral history, and the lived culture of the community, past and present. This is illustrated by many of the "songs of exile" of the 18th and 19th centuries in which Gaels spoke of their longing not just for the "land" of their birth, but also the community that was indistinguishable from it. In Gaelic-language culture and thought, there isn't a separation between the community and the land. Indeed, the "hills are alive" as the old song has it not with the sound of music but with the lives of those came before. When Gaels sang of their homeland, there was hardly a distinction made between the lives they lived there and the "there" – the place.

We can further see how the word's meaning expands beyond these bounds when we see that it is related to the word *dùthchas*, which means heredity, nationality, ethnicity, culture, instinct, and the adjective form can mean any or all of the meanings of endemic, indigenous, natural, native, traditional, or even the vernacular (language).

Let me make a generalization – at which some make take offense: Where the "English-language cultural" eye sees a landscape as an empty tract of land that is inhuman and of little worth unless it's exploited and a profit made from it, the Gaelic eye sees *dùthaich* – an area that is alive with human history, experience, and memory that is of value in and of itself because there is no separating the "natural" from the "human."

Following this, in Gaelic-language culture, the "environment" is not something existing separately from the lives of the people, nor does of the beauty of the landscape as just something to look upon inspire devotion. There is a word for the environment by itself – *àrainneachd* – and one for the community – *coimhearsnachd* – but these combine in all their implications, extensions, and ramifications, in the single word *dùthaich*.

Here, the retired professor pushes to the front with "learning objectives." From this short piece, I hope you've gained a greater understanding of the word *dùthaich*, and also an appreciation how that one word packs within it all that I've just written (and so much more).

Which, of course, would be impossible to cram into a pithy proverb!

There are a couple different ways we might regard this proverb. One is as an imperative – a kind of moral value that should be upheld. It's the right thing to do.

Another way to understand the proverb is in the sense of *you don't know where you are until you understand where you have come from*. This has to do with properly, which is to say more *completely*, understanding ourselves. Just as we understand ourselves individually by having insight into the experiences in our lives that shaped us as individuals. Part of those experiences are not just individual but also cultural, and so as members of a culture, we can better understand the forces that shaped our collective identity through "attachment" to the heritage of our ancestors.

As *dùthaich* can be understood to literally mean "land" – that is, the environment, or the earth – this proverb might also be understood as emphasizing the importance of preserving and the natural environment – that is, not polluting it, not degrading it, not despoiling it. But it's interesting and important that Gaelic phrases this idea not as maintaining a piece of property that we've inherited, but as having a "relationship" with it; important to point out, as well, that this dàimh that we are here urged to have, keep, maintain, is the same *dàimh* that refers to a personal relationship with the land that is to be nurtured and cared for the same as those relationships with our families, our friends, our loved ones, our fellow Gaels, and all other people.

Language Notes

Còir = right, proper

Dàimh = relationship, kinship, affinity

Against the rocks

Thèid dùthchas an aghaidh nan creag.

Heritage will go against the rocks.

One image this might suggest is that of mighty waves crashing against a cliff. Eventually, the waves (a metaphor for *dùthchas*, or heritage) will wear away even the rocks.

We might think of this as being illustrated as a tiny stream cutting its way through mountains, eventually etching a Grand Canyon. Just as water slowly erodes all that stands against it, one's heritage will wear away the stones and boulders that resist it, revealing the enduring strength and wisdom passed down through generations.

Language Notes

Dùthchas -- Here, again, we see this word, one that is very important in the consideration of Gaeldom.

thèid – the future tense of the irregular verb *rach* ("to go" in English). Unlike English, Gaelic as a "true" future tense, whereas what we call the future tense in English is actually what linguists call a future *aspect* in that it requires a 'helping' or auxiliary verb (as in **will** *go*). You might think of the Gaelic future tense as corresponding with the past tense, as in English we can refer to a past action with a true past tense, such as *went*. Well, Gaelic has a future tense that mirrors that form. I know, TMI ...

an aghaidh – translated as "against," the expression is very visceral as it literally means "in the face."

To speak imperfectly

Nas fheàrr a' Ghàidhlig bhriste na Bheurla chliste!

Better broken Gaelic than fluent English

A sentiment that is contested by some. There are language purists in any language who hold to the idea that the use of language should be free of all errors in grammar and vocabulary, not to mention pronunciation. But nowadays, considering the perilous state of Gaelic (which is considered an endangered language), and the shrinking number of people who are acquiring the language *on ghlùin* – from the knee, that is, as a native language as children – and considering the historical *mi-rùn mòr nan Gall* – the great hatred for Gaelic by the non-Gael that has pervaded English-speaking society and government for hundreds of years, and which has contributed to the decline of the vitality of the language, there might be something to be said for speaking "broken Gaelic" rather than not speaking it at all, for it is by first speaking brokenly that we come to be able to speak fluently.

But why is important to speak Gaelic at all? A couple of the following proverbs will expand upon the rationale that it is so.

Language Notes:

Nas fheàrr ... na ... better than

A' Ghàidhlig = "the" Gaelic, a common phrasing, extending even to English speakers in Scotland, who in English will sometimes refer to "the Gaelic."

na Bheurla = in English. Here, the expression is contracted from *anns a' Bheurla* – "in the English."

Bhriste = broken, inflected. Root word = *briste*

Chliste (root = cliste) -- fluent

Language as a part of *dùthaich*

'S mairg an duine a chaill a ghuth

**Woe to him who has lost his voice
Who has a stream of song
And who cannot sing it**

Donnchadh Mór ó Leamhnacht, Great
Duncan of Lennox, c. 16th century

Gaelic scholar Michael Newton writes,

To be in control of one's own narrative embodies self-
determination and self-realization. The contrary condition –
that of having no voice – represents a lack of power.

A people without a language

'S sluagh gun teanga sluagh gun anam.

A people without a tongue is a people without a soul.

Underscores the profound connection between language and cultural identity. Language is not merely a tool for communication; rather, it embodies the history, values, traditions, and collective memory of a people. Without their native tongue, a community loses its means of expressing its unique worldview and transmitting its heritage across generations. This loss erodes the cultural fabric and spiritual essence that bind individuals together, leading to a disconnection from their roots and a diminished sense of belonging. Thus, the extinction of a language represents not just the loss of words, but the silencing of a people's "voice," the extinguishing of a people's soul.

Use it or lose it

'S an cànan nach cleachdte teanga seacte

The language not practiced is a language withered.

This is true on both a personal level and a social/societal level. An individual who once was fluent in a language – even from birth – may forget large swaths of language – grammar, syntax, vocabulary if they don't use that language – very often because they move out of a social environment which employs it.

Likewise, a culture may "forget" its language, too. If the language is not passed along from generation to generation, if it is not used in the home, in the street, in official proceedings of government and society, in play and work – those functions of the language will gradually "wither" and eventually die.

The language loss can be so extreme that people even forget that they –
meaning, their ancestors – once spoke the language.

There are areas in Scotland which were once Gaelic, but in which people
who nowadays live claim that "Gaelic was never spoken here," even though
there are clear records of Gaelic having been spoken, and sometimes even the
names of the area are clearly Gaelic or Gaelic derived. For example, some
people in Ft. William in Scotland – the English name for *A' Ghearasdain* –
recently objected to the printing of bilingual road signs, claiming just that
same thing – despite being surrounded by towns and geography with clearly
Gaelic names and Gaelic-derived names: Loch Eil, Ben Nevis, Cairn Mor Dearg,
Aonach Beag!

I have encountered people at Highland Games – that is, *Gaelic*-inspired
festivities with events, competitions, and displays derived from the *Gaelic*
Highlands – who don't even know what Gaelic is. I was minding an
information tent once – *Learn about Gaelic Here* – and it was not uncommon
for people to come in and ask … *What's that? What's this Garlic of which you
speak?* To underline my point about cultural amnesia, these were people
enjoying and celebrating their heritage at the *Highland* Games (which some
have renamed "Scottish Festival") of which all if not most of the cultural
aspects are Gaelic-culture derived – the kilts, the bagpipes, the tossing of the
caber, the Highland dancing, not to leave out the *uisge-beatha* (whisky) and
the haggis!

Language Notes:

'S – It is common for the verb *Is* to be contracted, especially at the beginning
of a sentence. I can also note that Gaelic has two verbs that reflect
different meanings for "be" –

- **bi** – the "be" (is, are, was, etc.) which describes a quality of
something, or is used as a 'helping' verb, as in She **is** *kind, or We **are***
going to the beach.
- **Is**   the "be" which is called the assertive verb, in that it "asserts" that
one thing *is* another thing, as in *She **is** a doctor. Robert Burns **was** a*
poet.

The hardships

Cuimhnich air cruadal nan daoine bhon tàinig thu.

Thomas Faed, The Last of the Clan, 1865.

Remember the hardships of those from whom you came.

Related to the previous proverb: This painting by Thomas Faed memorializes the expulsion of Gaels from the Highlands, and their exile from the land of their ancestors to distant lands, including America, Australia, and New Zealand. The year 1785 was referred to by the Gaels as *Bliadhna nan Caorach* – the Year of the Sheep. The Highland Clearances was a process of eviction – or *clearing* -- of our ancestors from the land they and their forebearers had inhabited for more than a thousand years. The Clearances were often carried out by force – sometimes by burning highland cottages down over the heads of the people who lived in them. They came about as part of a changing system. The old system in which people were bound together in clans by kinship and reciprocal relationships and land was held in common for the welfare of the clan was replaced by a capitalist land-owning system -- sheep replaced the people because sheep were more profitable; people were cleared from the land to make way for hunting preserves because the Highland Gaels were disposable.

The proverb here is a little different from the preceding one. Whereas before, we were urged to remember our ancestors, here it is the hardships they endured that we are encouraged to remember, an admonition that is two-edged. Not only are we to remember them, but in remembering their hardships – and hopefully in that remembrance in some small way vicariously experience it, we may be moved to empathize with people today who endure hardships of prejudice, deprivation, exile, flight from persecution.

I've often thought that as part of keeping that memory alive, we should ritualistically recreate symbolically some aspect of the hardships of our ancestors. I'm not suggesting that we should yearly burn down our houses in remembrance of the evictions, but perhaps something as any one or a combination of any of the following might help keep the memory alive:

- **Fire ceremony**: Light candles or perform a controlled burning of a sprig of heather in remembrance of the burning out of the cottages of the Gaelic crofters to represent the displaced families and communities.

- **Create a cairn** -- or stack of stones, with each stone representing a cleared village or family. The creator of the seminal Gaelic dictionary Edward Dwelly writes of the custom of creating this informal monument in remembrance of the dead, from which arose

  > the saying "*cuiridh mi clach 'nad chàrn*," I will add a stone to your cairn, which betokens a friendly intention and means that one's remembrance shall be kept alive. When the remains of anyone were carried a long distance for interment and the bearers had to take some rest on the way, a cairn was put up there also and those who passed by were expected of their charity to put a stone on it and pray for the soul of the deceased. Cairns are still frequently erected to mark the spot in which a funeral has rested and on whatever spot a person is found dead, a few stones are immediately put together.

- **Recitation of names:** Read aloud names of displaced individuals, clans, or cleared settlements.
- **Symbolic walk:** Organize a solemn procession that symbolizes the course of eviction. Participants might "pack" symbolic representations of their belongings to carry with them as they are ritualistically "cleared" from their homes. Stop along the way to share a simple meal of bannocks or oatmeal cakes (and, as appropriate, a swig of *uisge-beatha*!).
- **Plant native Scottish flora** – heather, bluebells, thistle, bog myrtle, or gorse (& etc.) -- or trees (Scotch pine, alder, oak, elm, dogwood, or others) to symbolize resilience and renewal.
- **Have a cèilidh --** Share songs, music, histories, and personal family stories related to the Clearances.
- **Create a commemorative piece of art:** For those artistically inclined, craft a communal artwork depicting scenes or symbols of the Clearances.

All the water in the ocean

Cha nigh na tha dh' uisge 's a' mhuir ar càirdeas.

All the water in the sea won't wash out our kinship.

This one is intensely Gaelic, in its use of the same word, *càirdeas*, for "kinship" as is used for "friendship."

There are a number of ways we could understand this proverb.

One, on the surface, taking "all the water in the sea" to represent an immense and irresistible force, our kinship would withstand even that seemingly infinite power. We might understand this as a kind of sentimental hyperbole like "I love you more than a million dollars," or my love for you is "higher than the mountains, deeper than the sea."

But the expression is more than a cheap exaggeration, because it goes deeper than our feelings about our relationship. It refers to the fundamental truth that our "kinship" is one of culture, history, shared personal experiences, as well as historical. And in this, in some ways, even to our DNA.

And if you wanted to go even deeper, I guess we could say this about our kinship with all humans, and then, our kinship with all living things.

The sweetest music

Am fear as fhaide a chaidh on taigh, 's an ceòl a bu bhinne a chual e riamh "tiugainn dhachaidh."

To him who has gone farthest away, the sweetest music he ever heard was "Come home."

In today's often disconnected world, especially in the West where people frequently move multiple times during their lives, shifting to new neighborhoods and bigger, "better" houses, we might lose sight of the importance of our home communities, which fostered us and nurtured us when we were young, which provide a touchstone for our cultural identities, and which lend us strength and support during times of trouble.

Neither can we ignore the tendency of people in a stable community to preserve and protect their natural environment – perhaps more so than people who are just passing through until they make enough money to move someplace "better" or more prestigious. So, in a way, one of the things that this proverb enforces is the preservation of the home environment – both cultural and natural.

Language Notes

Am fear as fhaide – Here we see the flexibility of Gaelic syntax with the shift to the front of the sentence *am fear as fhaide on taigh a chaidh* ("the one farthest from home has gone). There are other ways to state this idea, but this structure serves to emphasize the focus of the sentence.

an ceòl a bu bhinne – literally, "the music that *was* sweetest" (the sweetest music). One of the many unique features of Gaelic is that comparative adjectives (one thing is better, best, bigger, biggest, etc. must be given a tense (past or present) much like a verb. So, in this case, you can't say "the music that is the sweetest I ever heard ..." (not grammatically, anyway). When I mentioned this requirement of Gaelic to a linguistics professor once, he expressed surprise. Although he was fluent in more than one Asian language, moderately competent in several European languages, and knowledgeable of languages in general, he'd never heard of such a thing!

Children of the Gael!

Clanna nan Gaidheal 'an guaillibh a chèile!

The children of the Gael shoulder to shoulder!

One of the best known and most often quoted of all Gaelic sayings. Literally it is ' in each other's shoulders,' i.e., each with his arm round the shoulder of the other, as Highlanders would do in crossing a deep or fierce water together.

This reminds us that Gaelic culture was (and is) a *collectivist* rather than an individualistic culture – a "we" culture, rather than an "I" culture -- which makes sense especially in our present context in that if we are to preserve our heritage and our language, it must be *together* that we do so. (One can't speak a language all by oneself!)

"Children of the Gael" is a quite common phrasing, which reminds us that one of the meanings of the word *clann* ("clan") – the prototypical social unit of Gaelic culture – is also "children."

Sociologists sometimes typify a culture by whether it is an "I" culture or a "we" culture. I-cultures tend to emphasize the individual, the rights of the individual, the needs and desires of the individual, with stronger ideas about personal boundaries and autonomy. While we-cultures tend to emphasize the group, obligations to the larger group and to others, responsibilities that people have to others, relationships rather than autonomy, stronger bonds of solidarity with others within the group. None of this is absolute or black-and-white; everything exists on a spectrum, but Western cultures tend to be more *I*-oriented, while Asian tend to be more *we*-centered.

However, that said, there is a strong *we*-component to Gaelic culture. This is seen in the proverbs that emphasize solidarity with others and relationships within the family and the Gaelic community.

As a quick illustration, there are no Gaelic sayings to the effect of

- Every man for himself
- Look out for Number One
- It takes a good guy with a gun to stop a bad guy with a gun (with its implications of the exaltation of the individual hero and the rejection of any collective action)

The collector of Gaelic proverbs Alexander Nicolson does quote this expression:

- An uair a bhios rud a dhith air Dòmhnaill, gheibh e fhèin e.
  - When Donald wants anything, he'll get it himself.

But "Donald" here is not admired in Gaelic culture, as Nicolson adds, "Donald represents the pushing man who will not be over-nice in helping himself to what he wants. "*Dòmhnall dhà fhèin*" – Donald for himself -- is a somewhat similar phrase.

Which is not to say that Gaelic culture emphasizes the complete abnegation of the self. For instance,

- Am fear nach toir an aire dha fhèin, bidh càch a fanaid air.
  - He that cares not for himself will be mocked.

But even here, the focus is just as much on how one appears to others -- how one stands in relationship to others – just as much as on selfish self-care or isolationist self-reliance.

There is a reflection of this aspect of collectivist orientation in the emigration patterns of the 1700s and 1800s, when many Gaels were forced – either because of economic conditions or because of mass eviction – to leave the Highlands. It was not uncommon for them not to emigrate individually, but as a group – as a whole village or even a whole clan -- sometimes building farming villages in the New World that replicated the villages in the homeland – even to the ordering of houses of the individual families.

without a brother to lean on

Is lag a' ghualainn gun bhràthair.

Weak is the shoulder without a brother.

The song by Bill Withers goes

> Sometimes in our lives
> We all have pain
> We all have sorrow
>
> Lean on me
> When you're not strong
> And I'll be your friend
> I'll help you carry on...

Again, with the shoulders! "No man is an island," as the English poet John Dunne wrote, and so it is with Gaels – the recognition that we are all interdependent upon one another is baked into the culture.

Illustrations abound throughout history that attest to the truth of this observation: Important achievements have come about because of the "band of brothers" (and sometimes, sisters) who worked together, rather than through the efforts of a lone hermit in a cave.

No general ever won a war by himself; every soldier who fought by his side contributed to the victory. Robert the Bruce was a valiant leader in the fight for Scottish Independence, but he could not have beaten the armies of the English tyrant without the other Scots who followed him. The United States was created upon the shoulders of the founding *fathers*, many people who worked and fought together.

The American Civil Rights movement, which achieved greater rights for millions of people, was the result of shared efforts and the networks of activists. Other major social changes, like women's suffrage or rights of working people not to be abused or exploited, were achieved through the collective efforts of many individuals supporting each other.

Alexander Fleming made the breakthrough discovery about the antibiotic properties of penicillin, but it was countless other scientists and business people who together developed the original microbe into a viable, life-saving medicine, and distributed it around the world.

The astronauts who walked on the moon were able to do so because of the teams of engineers and scientists who contributed to that achievement. Steve Jobs depended upon his collaboration with Steve Wozniak in the creation of Apple Computer.

Even from a purely personal perspective, emotional and social ties make us more resilient, enable us to live longer and healthier, foster our ability to cope with stress, encourage us in our striving to fulfil our goals.

creating community

Coinnichidh na daoine ged nach coinnich na cnuic.

People may meet, but mountains never

A speaker at a recent Royal National Mòd quoted this seanfhacal. In other words, people can move "towards" each other and create a community. While "mountains" represent the immovable and insentient. in that they are stationary and isolated, humans have the capability to form relationships and connect across distances – whether that distance is next door or on the next continent, or whether it is a distance of time as long ago as yesterday or decades ago.

This aphorism was spoken in the context of a coming together of Gaelic people at the *Mòd* – many of whom had never met before, but were congregating to share their culture and their history as a people – in a word, referring to the previous proverb -- their *kinship*. Sometimes, after having been separated for hundreds of years, for the Mòd is a gathering of Gaelic people from all over the world, of Gaels and Scots from across the diaspora ... from all the lands where we have been scattered.

Language Notes:

Mòd – though originally meaning simply an "assembly" or a "gathering," nowadays the word most often refers to a Gaelic cultural festival that celebrates the Gaelic arts of language (poetry, storytelling), music (singing, piping, fiddling), and dance (individual Highland dancing and group forms such as reels); these are often performed in a competitive format, with awards given. The most famous, or the central Mòd is the Royal National Mòd that takes place yearly in Scotland, but these events are held around the world in regional Mòds.

No man is an island

Cha duine duine na h-aonar.

A person alone is no person / A person is not a
person by themselves (that is, in isolation).

Language Notes:

Cha duine duine . Literally, "not a man a man ..." How does that make sense?
Where's the verb? Well, a couple things going on here:

- Gaelic has two words that translate as "to be" in English.
  - One is the word that is used to describe (mostly) either a
    quality as in *Tha e àrd* (He is tall), or is used as a "helping
    verb" – *Tha i a' bruidhinn* (She is speaking.)

- o To say that one *thing* is another *thing*, (most of the time) we have to use what is known as the assertive verb – *Is* (which translates as 'to be' in English, but only for some uses).
    - ’S mise Mìcheal -- I am Michael
    - ’S Fred Finkelthorpe an dotair – Fred Finkelthorpe is the doctor. (*’S* is the contracted form of the assertive verb *Is*.)
- But, in this expression, where is the *Is* (or the *’S*) – the verb? The answer is that in the negative (as here), the *Is* is ellipsed – that is, it's there, but you can't see it. It's assumed. So, while it looks like the sentence doesn't have a verb, it really does! It's just invisible! (The incredible Invisible Gaelic Verb!)

alone

Chan fhiach duine na aonar.

A man by himself is worthless.

(figuratively): It is not good that a person should be alone.

A corollary to, or an alternate phrasing, of the preceding expression, this axiom reflects the emphasis in Gaelic culture on community, interdependence, and collaboration.

We can unpack this thusly: What some scholars refer to as *the myth of the individual* is not a Gaelic one. In fact. the ideology is in direct opposition to Gaelic culture. As scholar and poet Meg Bateman pointed out, even the genre of auto-biography in Gaelic culture misses the one thing that would seem to be required – and that is the *auto* part, the subject of the biography, in many cases focusing more on the community than on the person.

In addition to that, history, experience, and even the environment have enforced the necessity of cooperating. In alignment with the proverb *an guaillibh a' chèile* -- shoulder to shoulder -- this proverb entails the observation that all human achievement has come about through collaboration, for in the Gaelic experience, what is called "individualism" really only benefits those who are already rich and powerful. Bill Gates, Elon Musk, Jeff Bezos, and the like, can afford to be "individuals" – being so wealthy, and in our culture therefore so powerful, that they are impervious to most of the trials and tribulations that visit those with less wealth.

The Gaelic experience, however, is one in which the great mass of people suffered at the hands of such "individuals": men who bought the land the people and their communities lived on and evicted the inhabitants so they could develop hunting reserves, or so they could bring in sheep, which they thought were of much more value than the people who lived there before.

One example of the power of working together can be seen in the Crofter's Movement of the late 1800s. After nearly a century of being victimized by landowners, of being evicted from their dùthaich, sometimes even being forced to leave their homeland and emigrate to foreign shores – either by the descendants of the chiefs who used to protect them, or by foreign capitalists who had purchased the land of the people's ancestors as investments (or sometimes, hunting reserves) -- banding together, the Crofters of the *Gàidhealtachd* won security in their tenure on the land of their ancestors. They also won the right to unite as a community and buy the land from the land owners. Even today, many Highland communities have bought their own land and govern the territory within their domain as cooperatives.

Wresting rights and power from the powerful was not something that one person could do alone – for indeed, one person alone was of little worth in such a struggle.

Following this, much of Gaelic culture is not one that adores wealth and power, but one that has sprouted from the ground up. The 19th century collector of Gaelic folklore, Alexander Carmichael, reports the material condition of the home of one of his prime sources. It was, he wrote, about fifteen feet long, ten feet broad, and five feet high. There was nothing in it that the vilest thief in the lowest slum would condescend to steal.

For a people and their culture to endure in such an environment and in such conditions, sticking together would be more important and of more benefit than going it alone.

While we have to be careful about essentializing, or stereotyping – that is, thinking that everybody in a culture, or a society, or a nation, or a country, or a race, or an ethnicity does this or that, behaves in such a such way, believes in one thing or another, there are such things as cultural tendencies, which might be one of the rationales for referring to a "culture" in the first place.

That said, we might raise the question, *what do the proverbs tell us about what is valued in Gaelic culture?*

it comes to all

Nuair a thig e air duine thig e air uile

When it comes to one, it will come on everyone

No storm hits only one house.

Gaelic culture tends to emphasize the collective circumstances – either the shared tragedy or well-being of the community. This tendency goes so deeply that Meg Bateman, the renown Gaelic poet and scholar, commenting on the Gaelic novel *Deireadh an Fhoghair*, wrote of the absence of the individual in Gaelic autobiography – that is, strangely to many people in other Western cultures, Gaelic autobiography tends to focus on the *coimhearsnachd* – the community -- rather than the individual person.

This proverb suggests in many ways that what one person experiences very often has broader social implications. For example, the COVID-19 epidemic began as a simple infection of a virus thought to have been lodged in bats in a far-away Chinese city. But within a short period of time, what began as one man's illness spread to the entire world. Many women have experienced sexual assault or sexual abuse, but many victims thought that they were alone. It wasn't until the #METOO movement brought to light the shared experience of many women that we as a society realized that what had been passed off before as isolated incidents were actually part of a much wider epidemic of social pathology. Many children have been abused by trusted counselors – teachers, ministers, priests, Boy Scout leaders – and for too long, each abused child suffered in silence, thinking they alone experienced a singular, unique pain, and they carried that aloneness as a shame.

But we've come to understand that what happened to one actually impacted us all. We're reminded of the oft-quoted aphorism attributed to Martin Niemöller, in which he referred to the elimination of political enemies by the Nazis during the holocaust – made possible in part by many people's thinking atomistically, of not seeing the bigger, shared picture. Of thinking, *Well, bad day for you, but it doesn't have anything to do with **me**.*

> First they came for the socialists, and I did not speak out—because I was not a socialist.
>
> Then they came for the trade unionists, and I did not speak out—because I was not a trade unionist.
>
> Then they came for the Jews, and I did not speak out—because I was not a Jew.
>
> Then they came for me—and there was no one left to speak for me.

While it is true that sometimes events – tragedies, atrocities, even – are "one-offs," that is, they happen to one person only, as many other Gaelic proverbs remind us, we are not atoms, spinning in a void of space in isolation, but we are related by an interconnecting web.

It's impossible for a fly to touch one strand of that web without the tremor reverberating throughout the entire network.

In the same way, the evictions from ancestral lands that became known collectively as the Highland Clearances were not inflicted upon only one family by only one evil landlord but were like a storm that swept across a whole *dùthaich*, the entire Gàidhealtachd, and its entire population.

What happened to one, happened to all, for even those who weren't evicted themselves experienced the reverberations of that terrible time.

Work and Success

knowledge and education

'S trom an t-eallach an t-aineolas

Ignorance is a heavy burden.
(Compare to the English, "Ignorance is bliss.")

Certainly, we can apply this bit of wisdom to our contemporary lives: Would you go to a doctor who failed his medical board exam? How about one who doesn't believe in germs and doesn't wash his hands before examining you? Nowadays, such a practice constitutes simple common sense, but it wasn't that long ago that even physicians didn't wash their hands – even after dissecting corpses – and subsequently rather than cure diseases actually were responsible for spreading them. Aside from those people who get their medical advice from talk-show hosts with barely a high school diploma, it would be wise to stick to those practitioners who actually know what they're doing, because the *burden* of ignorance in this case might very well be the patient's death.

In every day, less exulted terms, what about the person who is looking for a job and misses the opportunity for the job of her dreams for which she is perfectly qualified because she didn't know of the opening? The *burden* of her ignorance in this case is missing out on a life-changing career and remaining stuck in a job she hates.

In terms of the Gaelic experience, education has long been prized as one of the few ways to escape the poverty of the Highlands – either to move and live in more affluent areas of the country, or to return to one's home community as a professional.

Also, I can't help noting that this reverence for education and intellectual attainment extends beyond Gaelic culture into Scottish culture in general. In my visits to Scotland – *an dùthaich*, as it were – I noticed something that I eventually formulated as a rule: What a people truly value, they imprint on their money. And what I noticed was imprinted on the Scottish currency were pictures of poets, intellectuals, scientists, and others who had worked for the betterment of humanity. Right now, I have in a small frame over my desk a Scottish five-pound note with the picture of the poet Robert Burns on it. I have had pass through my hands currency with the images of such people as the novelist Sir Walter Scott, or the Scottish businesswoman Scottish businesswoman Kate Cranston, who, as the text on the 20-pound note reads, "She has created a need for just the right thing, in just the right way, at just the right price"; author Nan Shepard, with her quote "It's a grand thing to get leave to live"; educator Flora Stevenson; scientist Mary Somerville; the hero of Scottish independence, King Robert the Bruce; and in addition, a series of bank notes that memorialize Scottish wildlife – otters, salmon, read squirrels.

Language Notes

'S trom ... Literally, the syntax of the Gaelic phrasing is the equivalent of what would be in English, *Is heavy the burden of ignorance.* Let's unpack that:

- Gaelic allows a more varied structuring of a sentence than English does. English syntax – the way in which we order the parts of a sentence – is in some ways rigid. While English does allow the interpositioning of coordinating or modifying elements, essentially, we are left with the undeviating backbone of subject-verb-object construction such as we would see in "Ignorance is a heavy burden." English does not even allow for the slight rephrasing of "A heavy burden is ignorance," which is grammatically correct, but just *sounds* weird. Gaelic on the other hand allows more variety in how sentences are composed, and in that variation, it affords more room for emphasizing different parts of the idea. Even as simple a phrase as the above may be composed in different ways to place emphasis on a different part of the idea:

- o   *Tha eallach an aineolais trom* – The **burden** of ignorance is heavy.
- o   *'S trom an t-eallach an t-aineolas* – Is **heavy** the burden of ignorance.
- o   *'S e aineolas eallach trom a th' ann.* – It is **ignorance** (that is) a heavy burden.

persistence

Am fear a thèid a ghnàth a-mach le lìon, gheibh e iasg uaireigin.

He that goes out consistently with his net will eventually catch fish.

We hear of cynical commentary such as that attributed (though doubtfully) to Albert Einstein: "Insanity is doing the same thing over and over again and expecting different results." This observation from a certified genius would seem to contradict the idea of persistence, but not really, for properly applied, persistence is a guaranteed success maker. (If not "guaranteed," at least with a greater probability of eventual success than just giving up.)

A lion does not catch its prey everytime it hunts. It is only by persisting in its hunting that it manages to feed itself and the other members of its tribe. (And actually, it's the lioness that does the hunting.)

A fisherman does not really do the "same thing" over and over again. The old saying goes, you never step in the same river twice. If there's fish in the river, while you might not catch any one day, you will the next. In the case of the Gaelic islanders 'going out' with their net, the sea is constantly changing, the conditions are changing, so it's not the 'same thing over and over again.'

Aside from these hypothetical examples (which are real enough), there are countless real-life stories of people achieving success in their endeavors because of their persistence:

- Thomas Edison famously tried – and failed – a thousand times to devise a filament that would burn in a lightbulb. When asked if he was discouraged, he just said, "No, I now know a thousand ways it won't work." And he went on to discover the one way that the light bulb would work!
- Walt Disney's ideas for his cartoons were rejected more than 300 times. He was fired from a newspaper for "lacking creativity." It's only because he persisted that his genius delights and inspires countless millions (can we say billions?) today.
- No discussion of the genius of persistence in our context would be complete without including the story of Robert the Bruce. In his struggle for Scotland's independence, his armies were beaten, he was betrayed by other Scots who should have been his allies, and he was driven into hiding in the mountains, with only a handful of his most loyal followers. Despondent, despairing, famously – probably aprocryphally – he found himself in a poor crofter's hut staring up at the rough-hewn beams. There he saw a spider trying to throw its web from one beam to another.

As the poet Bernard Barton wrote,

> Six times his gossamery thread
> The wary spider threw;
> In vain the filmy line was sped,
> For powerless or untrue
> Each aim appeared, and back recoiled
> The patient insect, six times foiled,
> And yet unconquered still ...

One effort more, his seventh and last!
The hero hailed the sign!
And on the wished-for beam hung fast
That slender, silken line;
Slight as it was, his spirit caught
The more than omen, for his thought
The lesson well could trace,
    That Perseverance gains its goal,
    And Patience wins the race.

The Bruce, according to legend, was inspired by this example of success through persistence and went on – according to history – to finally achieve Scotland's independence from English rule.

Patience

Glac thusa foighidinn 's glacaidh tu iasg

Two Children Fishing in Scotland by Otto Leyde

Catch patience, and you will catch fish.

This *seanfhacal* compliments the preceding. Certainly, in some ways, this *patience* is very similar to *persistence* but might be different in this: Patience focuses not on the repetition of effort, but on the ability to endure waiting through what might seem to be interminable periods of inactivity. Patience is different from persistence not so much in that you are repeatedly faced with failure and rejection, but that your efforts have no result whatsoever. Which is why, perhaps, fishing offers us a great life lesson. Many times, our lives are filled with long periods of time sitting by the river bank just waiting for a fish to bite.

But don't give up, this proverb tells us. Have patience!

Language Notes

's – "and," short for *agus*. In older texts you might see it *'us,* or sometimes even as *is.*

glacaidh – "will catch." The simple future for the verb *glac*, "to catch." Note the distinction between the first word of the saying – *glac* – and this – *glacaidh*. Gaelic possesses a 'true' future tense (unlike English, which requires a helping verb, as in "*will* catch"). For regular verbs (which is all but ten of the Gaelic verbs), the future tense is formed by adding an *-idh* or (as in this case) an *-aidh* to the end of the root verb. (Kind of a mirror image of the formation of the English past tense for regular verbs, which is formed by adding an *-ed* to the end of the root verb.)

Great things achieved ...

Tha clach beag air clach beag a' lìonadh beàrnan mòr.

Little stone after little stone fills a great gap.

This proverb tells of the importance of consistent effort, even if each part of that effort is – taken singly – small.

For example, if somebody wishes to write a book, it's not necessary to write the entire book at one sitting; but if that wanna-be writer composes just one page a day, as the author Steven King once noted, by the end of a year, they'll have written a 365-page novel.

Writer Josh Kaufman noted that all it takes is 20 hours to learn anything, and not just to learn, but to *master*! Somebody else broke that time down – 10 minutes a day, little more than an hour a week and four hours a month, for five months. But look at the "small stones" we're talking about: 10 minutes a day! Somebody could do that between morning coffee and brushing their teeth!

Historically, too, great "gaps" have been filled with a succession of "small stones."

For example, in the United States, the emancipation of slaves was brought about by innumerable "small" efforts stretching over decades – from the unsung work of many abolitionists, to the more celebrated Harriet Tubman's underground railway, to the widely spread speeches and writings of Frederick Douglas, to the staunch determination of Abraham Lincoln during the Civil War. Each a "small stone" that filled the gap between the America's promise of freedom for all people and the reality.

The successful landing on the moon in 1969 was the result of a succession of "small stones" of gradual and incremental gains in our scientific and technological knowledge that finally enabled the great leap across space to the moon.

Over the past couple centuries, the Gaelic language has fended off extinction through a series of "small stones" that constituted the refusal of the Gaelic community to accept the demise of their beloved language and culture. Starting from the time little more than 100 years ago when Highland children were beaten for speaking Gaelic in school, to gradually gaining acceptance of Gaelic medium education, including Gaelic nursery schools, to the establishment of the first-ever Gaelic college *Sabhal Mòr Ostaig* in 1973, the expansion of the publication of Gaelic literature of all kinds, and now the development of Gaelic learning opportunities throughout the world, both formal, informal, paid and even for free as on the free language-learning website Duolingo.

Small stones, indeed!

Language Notes:

a' lìonadh / lìonar – both inflections of the verb "to fill."

> **a' lìonadh** -- The verbal noun, which in some cases works similar to the *-ing* (or gerund) form of the English verb as in "is filling" or "are filling" – although in this case, it is used to express the present tense

"fills." (Gaelic does not have a simple present tense, so most often the *-ing* form is used to express present action, as in "I am filling the gap.")

lìonar – the future tense of the **passive** verb "fill" – often meaning "will be filled," but as the future tense in Gaelic can also express habitual or continual action – something that always happens -- as here, we should understand this as "Great gaps are filled ..." not as those gaps are being filled right now, but as a rule, they are filled.

Gaelic has a number of ways to say that something is done, or was done, etc. Although other ways involve the use of 'helping verbs,' one of those – that we see here -- is to add *-ar* or *-ear* to the end of the root verb; in this instance, the root verb is *lìon* (to fill) and the passive future would be *lìon + ar* which gets us to *lìonar*.

Working together

'S e iomadh làmh a nì an obair aotrom.

Engraving of Scotswomen singing while waulking cloth, c. 1770

Many hands make light work.

When my children were little, I'd encourage them to complete chores together with this proverb. We'd all go out into the yard and do together what needed to be done there. After dinner, we'd all wash the dishes together. After either their mom or me (dad) went grocery shopping, I'd rally them to help bring all the groceries inside. When we finished with whatever task we'd taken on, I'd point out how easily and how quickly we'd completed it, and remind them, "'S e iomadh làmh a nì an obair aotrom."

There are a couple reasons that this proverb *does not lie.* One is, simply, that collectively, the labor-hours multiply according to the number of people working. Sometimes, the factor is exponential, as in five people working together is the equivalent not of 5-times the work but maybe (for illustration's sake) 10-times the work accomplished in a set period of time. So, if it takes one person an hour to do something, five people can do it in ten minutes. (I'm not a mathematician, so don't ding me on the calculation – it's just meant to be a hypothetical.)

Then, also, there's the point that however long the task takes, working together often just seems "lighter" because of the very fact that we're doing it *together*, rather than separately. This is certainly true in Gaelic culture, in which like in many "traditional" cultures, there was not always such a clear distinction between *work* and *play,* or time to *work* and time to *socialize.* as we structure such things in the modern world. Very often, these activities overlapped. Such was the case, famously, with "waulking the wool" – *luadh* in Gaelic – one of the final processes in the making of woollen cloth.

In this process, the woven fabric was stretched, pounded, and soaked to ultimately soften it and make it usable. This was performed by several people – "back in the day," almost exclusively by women – who sat opposite each other across a table or a board. In the process of waulking, they would entertain themselves by exchanging stories, bits of news, giving advice to each other, and most famously, by singing what is known as *waulking songs* – a form of musical and lyrical art known in Gaelic as *òrain luaidh* – which were partially remembered and recited and partially made up on the spot. The pounding of the wool provided the musical beat to the song. It was a time of great jollity, as well as of production of an invaluable necessity to Gaelic society. So many hands went into the "work," that it did indeed seem light!

(Look up "waulking song" on Youtube.com. Here's a fun one from the 1940s – if you can copy the link one way or another -- colorized for a modern audience: https://www.youtube.com/watch?v=bOIZC16Jtz8)

Language Notes

Syntax: 'S e = lit, *Is it* (*It is*) many a hand that makes the work light. The **'S** at the beginning of the sentence is a contraction for the assertive verb **IS** and creates a common structure in Gaelic – *It is* … something that …

nì – the simple future of the verb *dèan* (to make, or to do). The Gaelic future tense is also used to express the habitual or continuous, in the same sense as the present serves in English, as in the case of the proverb's translation.

Sowing and reaping

Am fear nach cuir sa Mhàrt cha bhuain e as t-Fhoghar.

He that doesn't sow in March will not reap in Autumn.

A proverb that offers both an observation of a truth and a guide for our action, this is obviously true in an agricultural context – farmers have to sow their seeds early in spring if they are to harvest at the end of summer and have food to last them through the winter. No crops are harvested if the farmer waits until the end of summer sow do their planting.

The expression works as a metaphor for other life activities, as well. If a young person wishes to reap the rewards of a fruitful work life when they're old, they need to sow the seeds of education and training when they're young, along with each month sowing the seeds of contributions to their pension or

401k funds. Only then, will they reap the fruits of a lifetime of preparation, saving, and labor in the autumn of their life.

In my career as a student and an educator, I learned that reaping the harvest of education results from starting at the very beginning of a course – studying and completing assignments from day one, that is, in the "spring" of the class. I've seen too many students fail because they waited until the night before the final to begin studying or tried to write a 20-page paper the day before it was due.

Investment advisors tell us that often the best strategy is not trying to snag the killer deal, but sowing seeds of investment little by little on a consistent basis to eventually reap a harvest in the autumn of one's life.

Language Notes

cuir – in its most common usage, translated as "put," but used as in this case to mean to "plant" (which you might see as being putting seeds in the ground). In its root form, cuir can also be used in the sense of "send" – as in to send a letter or e-mail. The word is also used in the construction of many phrasal verbs with meanings that run the gamet from *cuir air chuimhne* (remind, put into memory); to *cuir a dh'iarraidh* (send for), to one of my favorites -- *cuir a-mach* (throw up).

nach cuir – who will not plant.

- The future form of the word is cuiridh – will plant (send, etc.), as in *Cuiridh am fear* (the man will plant), but the Gaelic future **negative** reverts to the root form of the word, which in this case is *cuir*.
- And in speaking of the negative (or the "not"), the Gaelic negative takes a couple different forms.
    - The independent form – ***cha*** *cuir am fear* – the man will **not** plant
    - The dependent/relative form: *am fear* **nach** *cuir* – the man **who** will **not** plant

Stick to what you're doing

An uair a bhios sinn ri òrach, bitheamaid ri òrach.

'S nuair a bhios sinn ri maorach, bitheamaid ri maorach.

When we are seeking gold, let us be seeking gold;

And when we are seeking shellfish, let us be seeking shellfish.

One thing at a time, or, stick to your knitting: Wise advice to concentrate on one thing – the thing that you do well, perhaps, and not to scatter your energy and attention amongst many.

The history of business provides us with examples of the validity of this proverb. Harley-Davidson launched Harley-branded bottled water. Starbucks diversified into offering Starbucks-branded furniture. Both efforts were disasters. Bic pen – the cheap and disposable fountain pen manufacturer – once tried to expand into the luxury perfume business; which failed as perfume is a luxury item, not one that consumers want to associate with cheap and disposable. Speaking of mis-aimed perfume ventures, Harley-Davidson (again) launched its own perfume line during the 1990s, which it named (no doubt ironicallly, hoping to capture the counter-everything spirit of its brand) *eau de toilette,* which effort went directly into the toilet!

Language Notes

- **An uair** = nuair. *Nuair* is a contraction, an encapsulated history of which goes something like: *An uair* (the time) > *'n uair* > *nuair* = when

- (nuair a) **bhios** = the relative future or habitual of the verb. Gaelic inflects verbs differently if we are making a direct statement or constructing a relative clause (in this case, one following the conjunction nuair (when): ***bidh*** *sinn (we will be)* vs. *nuair a **bhios** sinn (**when** we will be)*.

- **Bitheamaid** = *let us be;* the first person plural command. Yet another inflection of the verb *be*.

- **Ri òrach / ri maorach** = ri + the verbal noun or a noun often means 'engaged in' / 'occupied in doing'; tha Seumas a-nis ri maorach = James is now [engaged in] fishing for shellfish (not necessarily that he's doing it right now at the moment); bha làn fhios aig na h-ùghdarrasan air na bha iad ris = the authorities were fully aware of what they were up to; bu chòir dhut a bhith ri do leasanan = you ought to be at your lessons (engaged in your lessons.

Experience & practice

'S e cleachdadh a nì teòmachd.

Experience makes expertness. (Practice makes perfect)

This is not just a cliché, for the proverb highlights a fact that modern science has confirmed: Practice, establishes neural pathways in the brain and muscles that lend to what we call "expertise." However, what the Gaelic word *cleachdadh* tells us is that it's not just doing the same thing over and over again, but engaging in mindful experience. "Practice" implies doing the same thing over and over again – like a bored ten-year-old sawing away at a violin -- but the Gaelic word *cleachdadh* takes the activity out of the mere academic repetition as its meaning is more at "use" and "experience," that is, in engaging in an activity in different scenarios, different levels of difficulty, and in "real-world" situations.

Author Josh Kaufman posits that learning is achievable with only 20 hours of applied experience. That's 10 minutes a day for four months! He's not saying you'll become an expert, but that you'll become knowledgeable *enough*. In fact, it's upon an observation something like this that the Internet app **Duolingo** is based. With this website (I have no affiliation with it), you can learn Gaelic with just 10 minutes of application per day. Now, of course, the longer you go, the more fluent you'll become – and perhaps even one day achieve mastery in the language of your ancestors. But a place to start any skill you wish to acquire is finding 10 minutes to engage in *cleachdadh* – using it, experiencing it, practicing it.

But more than that ...

And not just any practice

'S e iomradh an droch latha a nì latha math gu iomradh.

It's rowing of the bad day that makes the day good for rowing.

In other words, practice rowing in a rough sea, and soon the rough sea will seem calm to you. A proverb that may be applied to matters other than the rowing of a boat, and a truth attested to in many modern instances. For example, I once knew a champion college wrestler who practiced with bands of weights around his ankles to improve his footspeed. Sometimes, musicians will rehearse a difficult piece with the metronome paced faster than called for. Runners such as American distance runner Galen Rupp use high-altitude training to improve their performance and endurance. Some NFL players use underwater treadmills or conduct pool workouts to enhance their training by increasing resistance to "normal" movements. Goalkeepers in soccer and hockey sometimes train with dimmed lights to sharpen their reflexes and focus.

Values

What will last

Thig crìoch air an t-saoghal, ach mairidh ceòl 's gaol

The end of the world will come, but music and love
will endure

A couple things strike me about this proverb. As often as Gaelic thought turns to the starkly – even pessimistically – realistic, here we have a saying that is relentlessly positive. Beauty, love, art will endure even at the brink of the Apocalypse.

The proverb speaks to a couple of the primary values in Gaelic culture. As often as Gaels are depicted as or thought of as fierce, unrelenting warriors, there are few proverbs that express the "Highland warrior" as an ideal – in fact, you won't find any in this collection. In Gaelic praise songs, just as often as a chief was lauded for the staunchness of his fighting in protection of his kith and kin, he is praised for how kind he was, how gracious, generous, and hospitable he was.

And so, we have this folk saying that in a sense posits both music and love as existing outside of human expression or action or feeling, as if they are eternal qualities and values in and of themselves. Even at the end of the world, they will continue to exist. And all we can do in this sphere is aspire to them and seek to realize them.

Highland hospitality

Bhithinn cuid oidhche a' toirt dha ged a bhiodh ceann fir fon achlais aige.

I would give him a night's quarters, though he had
a man's head under his arm.

As Alexander Nicholson wrote, "Nothing could be more expressive than
this of the Highland culture of hospitality," though admittedly the proverb
might be a bit of an exaggerated expression of that culture – or maybe it's not
so much an exaggeration, for the great collector of Gaelic folktales, *Iain Òg Ìle*
– Young John of Islay, or I.F. Campbell, as he was known in English – recorded
a story in which a father rescues his son from the spell of an evil wizard by
refusing the wizard's hospitality of food and drink until the wizard gave up
the kidnapped son. Of this, Campbell wrote,

> The laws of hospitality were so imperative and overruled other considerations so supremely, that a host would be glad to grant almost *any* [emphasis added] request, if by so doing he might induce his guest to accept of his cheer. (*More West Highland Tales*, v. 1, 1994, p. 216).

There are many other stories of how deeply entrenched the culture of hospitality was amongst the Gaels. For example, once a couple of young men got into a fight, and one was killed by the other. The killer fled the victim's friends to the nearest castle and requested hospitality – which in this context meant protection and safety. The Chief of the castle readily granted sanctuary and protection, as was required by custom. And so strong were the laws surrounding the custom of hospitality that he honored that promise even when he discovered that the man he was protecting had killed his own son.

Another story concerns an ancestor of none other than the Scottish national poet, Robert Burns. Walter Campbell lived a couple hundred years before his famous poet descendent in a house that was called *Taigh an Uillt* – House of the Burn. At the time, bands of renegade bards roamed the Highlands, demanding hospitality from any well-to-do Chief they landed upon. These were bands of 10 – 20 men, who were not only large, fierce warriors, but were threatening in a much scarier way. If they were denied hospitality or if they found the hospitality they received was too stingy, they would write vicious satirical poems about that clan chief. Everyone was afraid of the shame that such satires would bring upon them that hardly anyone dared to refuse them.

One year, Walter Campbell was the victim of this horde of unwelcome guests. After a long time in his home, they were eating and drinking him out of house and home. Finally, having had enough, he killed them all.

All the Highlands were outraged! Scandalized!

But the uproar was not because Walter Campbell had murdered the poets (I guess, everybody knew they had it coming), but because in doing so, he had violated the sacred law of hospitality!

The uproar was so great that Campbell had to flee to the Lowlands, where he took the new name of Burnshouse (get it? *Taigh an Uillt* / House of the Burn / Burnshouse?).

Language Notes

Bhithinn – For the most part, Gaelic, like English, isolates the pronoun subject from the verb. For example,

- he is
- I will be

However, there is one instance in which Gaelic fuses the two – the subject and the verb – into one word. This is the first person conditional. So, where in Gaelic, you might say,

- Bidh mi – I will be, with the verb and the subject together

you would say,

- Bhithinn – I would be, with the verb and the subject represented by one word.

The same holds true for the first-person plural:

- Bidh sinn – we will be
- Bhitheamaid – we would be

All other verbs besides the verb *bi* (to be, in English) receive the same treatment.

- chluichinn – I would play
- ruitheamaid – we would run
- chuirinn – I would put

& etc.

Are you a man or a dog?

Is e duin' a nì, ach 's e cù a dh'innseas.

He is a man who does; he's a dog who tells.

Making allowances for traditional Gaelic culture, which was male-oriented to the point of being what many today would characterize as sexist (as were nearly all cultures in times past, and many still are), in the contemporary sense, we may read *duine* here as a person -- a full-fledged, responsible, respectable person. That being the case, the point here is to contrast the self-promotion of "telling" with what Gaelic culture considered proper conduct, which is *doing* without bragging about what you've done.

A braggart will get his come-uppance. Gaelic culture seems to not like boasting, reflecting a cultural tendency towards modesty and the inclination of Gaelic culture to defer to the group rather than exult the individual. This dislike of pushing oneself forward, of bragging, seems to be in contrast with the spirit of our contemporary age, which holds that a person *should* self-promote, *should* dance for the TikTok as it were, *should* post pictures on FaceBook ("Look at what I had for lunch!") -- even to the point of inflating and exaggerating their abilities and accomplishments.

Here I can tell a story on myself. Having been brought up in a culture that values self-promotion, partly because in contrast with those in which people know each or at least know of each other, in American society, you're always encountering new people who don't know who you are, and partly because the lead question for introductions in this society is typically, *what do you do?* (which can also be taken to mean, *what have you done?*), I made the mistake in a Gaelic class I was taking out of *Sabhal Mòr Ostaig* (the Gaelic college in Scotland) of rattling off my credentials, my achievements, my experience … which to my chagrin, I realized didn't go over well. Instead of impressing anyone I earned myself the reputation as a *bòstair* – a braggart, a boaster.

Oich! (oopsie) *Egg on my face!*

Language Notes

Duin' – The word spelled out completely is *duine*. It is very common in Gaelic to truncate the vowel ending of a word if the following word begins with (or, as in this case, is totally) another vowel. The way I think of it is that Gaelic vowels don't like to hang out with other vowels in different words (in the same word, that's fine). In other words, while the English speaker would have no issue with saying "*duine a nì*" (pronounced duun-ya a nee), the Gaelic speaker would find the abrupt stop and start of the side-by-side vowels to be awkward and inelegant.

Don't be a dung-beetle

Cho àrd 's a sheòlas an ceàrr-dubhan, 's ann sa chac a thuiteas e

As high as a dung beetle "sails," it's into the shit that he will fall

The proverb warns us against over-arching ambition, of attempting goals beyond our capacity to reach them or sustain them. For example, in the late 1600s, Scots witnessed people in other nations exploring the new lands of the Americas, and thought … why not us? Why can't Scotland have colonies like England, Spain, Portugal, even the Netherlands.

And so, the Darien Scheme was launched, which financed the establishment of a colony in Panama that would elevate Scotland to the status of a powerful trading nation by virtue of control of an overland route between the Atlantic and Pacific oceans – a sort of precursor to the eventual construction of the Panama Canal 200 years later.

So enthusiastic were the Scottish people about the venture that 20% of all money in circulation in Scotland was invested in the plan, which failed because of poor planning, tropical diseases, and sabotage by rival colonial powers, with the result that the Scottish nation was bankrupted and was forced to seek a "bail-out" from the English government at the cost of the Scottish parliament voting in favor of union with England in 1707 -- a real-life example of "sailing" too high and failing into a pile of shit.

Language Notes

Syntax: The proverb is stated in a somewhat convoluted order, which illustrates a couple features about Gaelic.

cho àrd a sheòlas -- as high that sails. *Sheòlas* is the future relative form. As discussed elsewhere, Gaelic has a different form for the future relative unlike English in which we might see the same form of the verb being used in both independent and dependent constructions, in contrast with Gaelic:

- he **will sail -- seòlaidh** e
- who **will sail --** a **sheòlas**

In the second clause, we don't have what we might think of as a "normal" order, which might be

- *tuitidh e anns a' chac* = he will fall into the shit

but Gaelic allows for a different construction (not that you couldn't do this in English, but it's not common as it is in Gaelic):

- *'s ann sa chac a thuiteas e* – it's into the shit that he will fall

's is the contracted form of the assertive verb ***is***, and here maintains the Gaelic grammatical rule that a sentence (or an independent clause) must begin with a verb.

a thuiteas e – like with ***a sheòlas,*** the relative future special form for the verb (not *tuitidh* as it would be for the 'straight' independent phrasing of the idea – in other words, *tuitidh e* -- he will fall)

Minor note: *sa chac*, contraction for *anns a' chac*

Generosity

Fialaidheachd don fhògarrach, 's cnàimhean briste don eucorach!!

Generosity to the exile, and broken bones to the oppressor!

The *seanfhacal* relates to a long history of Gaels being exiled from their native lands, either within Scotland or without. Perhaps clans falling out of favor of the king and being scattered by the central government; or being driven out by an enemy clan; or in the 18th & 19th century, being hunted by the British government or being cleared from the *dùthaich* of their ancestors by the landowners. Sometimes, it might refer to somebody on whom hard times had fallen and had been forced to a life of wandering and begging. At any rate, the ethic of the Gael was to afford *fialaidheachd 's coibhneas* – generosity and kindness – to such a person.

I can't help but think of how this proverb applies to circumstances in our own times, when so many fògarraich – exiles, refugees – are crisscrossing the globe fleeing persecution, war, hunger, oppression, and even genocide. And how our Gaelic proverb reminds us to provide them with generosity, and "broken bones" to those who oppress them.

Language Notes:

Fialaidheachd – generosity, hospitality; related to *fialaidh*, bountiful, free, generous, hospitable, liberal, openhanded,

Fògarrach – the exile, the one who has been banished, the outlaw

Eucorach – more than "oppressor," the word relates to "criminal," or evil-doer; the unrighteous one. Derivation – *eu-* a negative, like non- or un-; *corach* derived from *còir* = 1 right 2 justice 3 duty, obligation

A **happy home**

Taigh gun chù, gun chat, gun leanabh beag, taigh gun ghean, gun ghàire.

A house without a dog, without a cat, or without a child, is a house without cheerfulness or laughter.

The collector of Gaelic proverbs, Alexander Nicolson, writes this *sean fhacal* appears to be "purely native" in its celebration of a large household, extended not just to all generations, but even to the non-human members of the family. And while the way the idea is expressed might be original, it does seem similar in spirit at least to the observation by Russian writer Leo Tolstoy in his novel Anna Karenina: "All happy families are alike; each unhappy family is unhappy in its own way."

A little side-note: Keep in mind that this, as all the other proverbs in this collection, were composed in a time that was somewhat different than today. Although the specifics may differ from those times to these, we can still take the spirit of the idea.

Language Notes

Taigh gun chù … taigh gun ghean –The *Is* (or as it sometimes appears in its contracted form, *'S*) is eclipsed, that is, it disappears altogether – leaving the two noun phrases adjacent to each other without the appearance of an expressed connecting verb.

Beauty

'S e trì rudan a tha as bòidhche air an t-saoghal:

- ***long fo sheòl***
- ***gealach mhòr,***
- ***'s boreannach trom.***

Three things that are the most beautiful in the world:

- a ship under sail,
- a full moon,
- and a pregnant woman.

Beauty, we are told, is in the eye of the beholder, but more than in the eye of an individual, in the eye of a culture. The point here is not what an individual person might declare as the most beautiful thing they've ever seen, but what seems to be central to a culture, for different cultures have different ideas as to what constitutes beauty, and what a culture chooses to hold as beautiful is reflective of at least some of the values of the culture itself, which prompts the question, what does this proclamantion tell us about Gaelic culture?

The "full moon" might reflect several things about Gaelic culture besides an appreciation for any abstract beauty of the moon. Or, rather, perhaps the perception of beauty is a reflection of other attributes. For instance, with the custom of cattle raiding amongst the Highland Gaels, the light cast by the full moon illuminated many a nighttime cattle raid. A 17th century chief of the MacGregors was known as *Donnchadh Dubh na Gealaiche* – Black Duncan of the Moon – for his prowess in stealing cattle by the light of the moon. As well, perhaps there is something universal about the appreciation of the moon: One of two celestial bodies that are most apparent in the sky, with the moon being perhaps more so than the sun simply by virtue of how it visually contrasts with the dark night sky, and how it is ever changing, lending it to marking time, demarcating the seasons.

Perhaps this regard hearkens back to an ancient Celtic reverence for the moon, dating back to the age of the Druids in the time before the Gaels arrived. On the Isle of Lewis in the Outer Hebrides there stands an array of monoliths known as the Standing Stones of Calanish -- *Clachan Chalanais.* These are roughly the same age as the monument of Stonehedge, and their purpose just as mysterious, although one possibility that has been suggested is that they were used by the ancients to chart the course of the triune Goddess, represented by the moon; each year she would hover at the point of the array and on three successive nights seem to touch the tips of the three hills in the distance, successively in her three different guises: *a' Mhaighdean, a' Mhàthair, 's a' Chailleach* – the Maiden, the Mother, and the Old Woman.

Alexander Carmichael wrote that even in the 1800s, when Scotland was thoroughly Christianized, people in Scotland still made such observances to the full moon such as turning their rings on their fingers or bowing to the moon. Of course, in Gaelic Scotland, ancient pagan practices co-existed side-by-side with Christian beliefs without conflict, as exhibited in this prayer to that invokes both the Christian trinity and The Moon as a kind of deity itself.

A' Gheallach Mhòr

An ainm Spiorad Naomh nan
gras,
An ainm Athar na Cathrach
aigh,
An ainm Iosa a thug dhuinn am
bàs,
O! an ainm na Trì tha gar dion
's gach cas,
Ma's math a fhuair thu sinn an
nochd,
Seachd feàrr gum fàg thu sinn
gun iochd,
    A' Ghealaich gheal nan
    tràth,
    A' Ghealaich gheal nan
    tràth.[1]

The Full Moon

In name of the Holy Spirit of grace,
In name of the Father of the City
of peace,
In name of Jesus who took death
off us,
Oh! in name of the three who
shield us in every need,
If well thou hast found us tonight,
Seven times better mayest thou
    leave us without harm,
    Thou bright white Moon of
    the seasons,
    Bright white Moon of the
    seasons.

---

1 Carmichael, Alexander. (1900/1972). *Carmina Gadelica: Hymns and Incantations*. Edinburgh: Scottish Academic Press.

A Pregnant woman might seem clear enough, with Gaelic culture's emphasis on family, kinship, and geneology, and a sentiment that might be considered universal rather than unique, except for the fact that in contemporary Western culture, it might be unusual to encounter the idea that a pregnant woman is beautiful. How many times have we seen a mother-to-be on a magazine cover or displayed on a billboard? How many times have we read of women who have recently given birth striving to shed all physical signs of having done so?

In both these cases, it might be interesting to research parallel declarations in different cultures: What do different cultures across the world consider to be most beautiful? While Gaelic culture spreads its net wide in its declaration of what is most beautiful, a casual Google search turns up articles focused on beautiful young women – the differences marked being that of skin color, body composition, and the like, though the beauty which is celebrated is in actuality pretty narrowly defined. There are Biblical passages which contrast inner beauty with outer – however, that is somewhat changing the topic. Likewise, there are several different quotes by *individuals* opining about "real" beauty, and these are inspiring, but more often than not, these quotes are in contrast to the culture's dominent perceptions of beauty.

What does a culture celebrate as being most beautiful, most valued? Some cultures value thinness, others full-figured women; some value body ornamentation; some focus on breasts, others on ankles, still others on the nape of the neck. Yet all these are similar in that they focus on the beauty of young women. If an anthropologist from Alpha Centuri were to ask that question of contemporary Western culture by researching depictions of ideas of beauty in contemporary Western media, they might say: fast (red) cars, extravagent wealth, "sexy" (but decidedly not pregnant) half-clothed women under the age of 25, and violence.

But nowhere would our researcher find a culturally-central statement such as this from the Gaelic.

With **ship under sail**, we move from the natural world to the material culture of traditional Gaeldom: We could look to the importance of sailing ships to the material culture of the Gaelic experience on the West Coast of Scotland. We should remember that for the Gaels in the Hebrides and the West coast, the highway of the sea was the primary means of getting from one place to another. Bearing in mind the absence of roads, the rugged and often inaccessible terrain, the ocean and the numerous inlets on the rugged coast provided the most accessible, least troublesome method of transportation.

Sailing ships represented commerce, linkage of communities, and considering the dependence of many coastal and island communities on fishing, sustenance. In some ways, the *bìrlinn* – the sailing vessel resembling a viking ship – was the SUV of its day (centuries ago).

Songs were song in praise of a chief – or, very often the son of a chief – and his splendid sailing ship. For example, "Seallaibh Curaich Eòghainn" which invites us to simply admire Eòghainn's *corrach* – small ship (though not that small as it had "còig ràimh fhichead oirre" – 25 oars).

There are many folk songs of lovers eloping – or attempting to elope – via ship. For instance, in the song "Chuir m' athair mise dhan taigh charraideach" (My father sent me to the house of sorrows), a young woman writes of her forced marriage and failed attempt at running away with her own true love, but as she laments to him,

> Tha do bhàta nochd 's na portaibh.
> Och, ma tha, chan eil i socair
>
> Your boat tonight is in the port
> Oh! but it's not calm (i.e., the weather)

and the young lovers are unable to get away. (Kind of equivalent these days to teenage lovers trying to escape a controlling father, but the car runs out of gas.)

The importance of the birlinn – or viking-type ship – is memorialized in the coat of arms of the Lords of the Isles, the independent (or semi-autonomous) kingdom that lasted for several hundred years during the middle ages.

Concepts of beauty often flow from the "practical." Here, what is represented by the ship is not some abstracted concept but rather – to be blunt – power, military might, independence, patriotic pride in the kingdom represented by the Lordship. The birlinn was kind of the equivalent of the modern tank, supersonic fighter, and bomber jet all rolled into one: in the Isles, the most sophisticated fighting engine of its day.

An early coat of arms of the Lord of the Isles, with the birlinn and the rising eagle of the MacDonalds displayed.

(If you still have a question about the significance of an item being represented in story and song, consider by way of comparison how many American stories celebrate the *car* – from road movies, to car chases being obligatory in nearly every adventure film, to a whole series of movies dedicated to cars being fast, furious, furiouser, and turbo charged!)

The corrupting influence of having too much

Is miosa na 'n uireasbhaidh tuilleadh 's a choir.

Too much is worse than want (that is, than 'too little').

Isn't this interesting! Whereas in much of present-day Western culture, wealth is celebrated to such an extent that billionaires complain about being asked to contribute to the common good, continuously wrangle ways to avoid paying any taxes at all, and conspire to lower the wages of their workers in order to increase the unfathomable pile of wealth they have accumulated – sometimes moving their profit-making factories out of higher wage communities and into poorer ones across the world -- here we have an expression that *enough is enough*.

Similar to the English expression that that "power corrupts" is this observation that having too much *wealth* – that is, economic power -- corrupts. Certainly, a different perspective on riches than the one that predominates much of the value system in today's Western world, a value system that celebrates billionaires simply for being rich, quite apart from what good they do with their vast wealth, that argues those who have the most should contribute the least to the common good, and that seeks to put as little restraint on the abuses of economic power as possible.

The Gaelic wariness of economic excess might have arisen from numerous sources: the shared poverty of the Gaelic people; the experience of being oppressed not just by military forces of more powerful nations, but also exploited by those more powerful economically; one dark example of which is the expulsion of Highlanders from their ancestral lands during what is known as the na Fuadaichean – the "evictions," or the Highland Clearances.

Here's a possibility of the type of experience that might have generated such a sentiment:

Caisteal Dhùn Robain -- Dunrobin Castle – is situated on the east coast of Sutherland in the north of Scotland. It is a popular tourist destination, presenting a splendiferous example of Scottish Baronial Style architecture that in this form may remind people of a mini-Versailles palace. It was certainly constructed, expanded, furbished and re-furbished to ostentatiously display wealth and claim prestige.

It was the home of Elizabeth, Duchess of Sutherland, one of the more notorious perpetrators of "clearing" the lands which she controlled of tenants. The "castle" displays ostentatious wealth …

... at a time when many Gaels lived much more modestly in cottages that were often dirt-floored.

Interior of a Highland Cottage, James Trout Walton

The grounds of the "castle" also contain a "hunting lodge" in which are displayed the stuffed and preserved bodies of animals – often rare or endangered -- which the owners were proud to have killed.

Little noticed, not as popular, not as spectacular, not far from the "castle" is a memorial which commemorates the flight of Highlanders during the Clearances – people who were forced from their little cottages so wealthy landowners could build luxurious palaces for themselves.

One Gaelic poet reflected on a visit to *Dùnrobain*, on the family which constructed it, and on the evil deeds they perpetrated thusly. It reads in part:

Beachdan air turas dha Dùn Robain	**Reflections on visiting Dunrobin Castle**
Cha b' urrainn dhomh cuimhnich a shealltainn No air na muinntir aon smuaintean no mun fhulangais aca an do thog na bailtean -- na bochda Dhùin Robain,	I could see hardly any memory of the people nor of the suffering that raised these towers -- the poor people of Dunrobin,
no air na taighean aca os an cinn an losgadh, 's iad air an fuadachadh gu borb -- chaidh a chanadh "ath-leasachadh" leis a' Bhana-phrionnsa Dhùin Robain.	their houses burned over their heads and they barbarously driven out in what was called "improvements" by the Princess of Dunrobin.
B' ann le sùilean ùra a chunnaic mi na stòrasan mìorbhailteach a chàrn i - na spùinnean nach mholainn -- na h-uabhasan Dùn Robain.	With new eyes I saw the marvellous treasures she piled up the stolen loot I could not praise that were the horrors of Dunrobin.
B' ann cho geal ri cnàmhan lìomhte a chaidh gu duslach a phronnadh 's an uair sin an tàthadh bha na mùirean Dùn Robain.	As white as polished bones pounded to dust and then into cement were the towers of Dunrobin,

Language Notes

A long piece, so a reminder of what started all this:

Is miosa na 'n uireasbhaidh tuilleadh 's a choir.
Too much is worse than want (that is, than 'too little').

Is miosa -- Here we see the assertive verb *Is* ("to be") used with the comparative *miosa* / worse.

syntax – Literally (or something approaching "literally") – "*Is worse than poverty more than enough.*" And though the expression "tuilleadh 's a chòir" is often translated as *more than enough*, we might look at the meaning of the word "coir," which should be understood as meaning *right, decent, fitting, virtuous, honest.* So, the expression might be better understood, at least in part, as signifying not "more than is enough" – if *enough* is taken to mean something like enough to satisfy needs, but rather "more than is decent."

Where English would separate the two parts of the comparative – *too much* **is** *worse than too little*, Gaelic syntax puts what in English would be the second half of the comparative (too much) first, and what in English would be the second part (too little) first; and since the verb comes at the beginning of the sentence, the two parts sit right next to each other in direct contrast. Literally, the sentence reads something like *Is worse than too little too much*

The ultimate value

Is cliùitich' an onair na 'n t-òr.

Honor is nobler than gold.

A sentiment that is not unique to Gaelic culture. Examples from cultures all around the world abound.

Historically, Socrates chose to die rather than compromise his integrity. In literature, the main character in the novel *To Kill a Mockingbird*, stood firm for what he believed against the mocking and ostracism of his racist neighbors. More recently the activist Malala Yousafzai suffered near-death violence in her advocacy of education for girls in her native Pakistan.

In our own Gaelic context, a famous example is to be had in the aftermath of the '45 rebellion and the Battle of Culloden Moor – *Blàr Chùil Lodair* in Gaelic -- which saw Bonnie Prince Charlie fleeing for his life from the soldiers of the British government. As the Prince hid in the mountains of the Highlands, the English King put a reward on his head of £30,000, which was the equivalent of more than $2,000,000 today, which considering the abject poverty many Gaels lived in at the time, was even more enormous than we can imagine.

Across the Highlands and the Islands for a full five months, Prince Charles fled the army which would have taken him back to London to be hanged as a "traitor." Sometimes he was just steps ahead of his pursuers, as when Flora MacDonald disguised him as her maid "Betty Burke," and he slipped through a redcoat checkpoint.

Yet, though many Highlanders knew the whereabouts of the Prince, not one betrayed him, and many helped him, not only losing the opportunity of great wealth, but at risk of their own lives if they were found out, for they accounted the honor of adhering in their loyalty more valuable than the wealth they might receive for betraying their Prince.

Truth and gold

Is fheàrr an fhirinn na 'n t-òr.

Truth is better than gold.

A proverb that explicitly asserts the value of truth over expediency and profit. The Gaelic hero Fionn resolved not to marry any woman who couldn't answer the questions he asked of her to test her wisdom. He posed a series of riddles to any number of women, and finally, he married Graidne because she could untangle them. One of the questions she answered was the riddle,

"De nas gile nan sneachd?" fhreagairt e.

"What is whiter than snow?" he asked.

"Tha 'n fhirinn," thuirt i.

"Truth," she answered.

We should pause for a moment and consider how alien this sentiment is to many people in our time, when politicians lie freely to such an extent that *fact checking* is even a thing: We can't count on those who would hold positions of the highest trust to tell the truth without having a researcher over their shoulder looking up whether what they say is the *truth, mostly the truth, or a pants-on-fire lie*; and even their supporters can do no better than weasel out of the accusation of lying by claiming *alternative truth*.

A corrolary to this proverb

Is fheàrr a bhi bochd na bhi briagach.

Better be poor than be deceitful.

Too often we learn of people of power and prominence lying to achieve gain:

- Financial fraudsters declare assets are worth more when seeking to borrow money from banks on them, and declare the same assets as worth less when paying taxes on them.
- Elizabeth Holmes, the founder of Theranos, falsely claimed that her company had developed revolutionary blood testing technology. In reality, the technology was flawed and unreliable. This deception led to significant investments from high-profile individuals and institutions before the truth was revealed, her corporation went bankrupt, and she was sentenced to prison.
- Bernie Madoff orchestrated one of the largest Ponzi schemes in history. He falsely reported consistently high returns to investors, using new investments to pay off earlier investors. This scheme collapsed in 2008, leading to massive financial losses – and sometimes ruination -- for thousands of people, and the eventual suicide of his son, who had long trusted his father was telling the truth.

In each one of these cases, the perps would have been better off, our society would have been better off if they had adhered to the Gaelic *seanfhacal.*

True riches

Na toir breith a-rèir coltais; faodaidh cridhe beairteach a bhith fo chòta bochd.

Don't judge by appearance: a rich heart may be under a poor coat.

The Scottish poet Robert Burns (who, some have argued, had a Gaelic heritage) in his poem "A Man's a Man for a' That" wrote of the superiority of the quality of a person over their social position and their riches:

> The honest man, tho' e'er sae poor,
> Is king o' men for a' that.

> In contemporary English:
> The honest man, though ever so poor
> Is king of men for all that.

Language Notes

Na toir breith – (don't judge. Literally, don't give judgment). The Gaelic imperative is formed from the root of the verb, and the negative by preceding it with *na*. However, the verb in question here – *thoir* – is irregular, and the negative future does not conform to the rule for regular verbs. So while with a regular verb – *cuir* (put), for instance -- we would see

- *cuir* = to put (the root verb)
- *cuir* = put! (command)
- *na cuir* – don't put! (command)

thoir does not follow that pattern. It's irregular!

Wisdom

Judging by appearances

Gille luideagach is loth pheallagach --

dithis nach bu chòir tàire a dhèanamh orra

A raggedy boy and a shaggy filly – neither should be scorned.

Or, the English-language expression, *Don't judge a book by its cover.* Perhaps, more broadly, this is a reminder that not only should we not judge by appearances, but we shouldn't judge by the present situation, for we never know how that situation will change and what will become.

Language Notes

The structure of the proverb illustrates the flexibility of Gaelic syntax. Let's take a look at it. As close as we can get in English and still remain intelligible:

- Gille luideagach is loth pheallagach -- dithis nach bu chòir tàire a dhèanamh orra
- A boy raggedy and a filly shaggy – both that should not scorn be made on.

Usually, Gaelic sentences are structured as to be verb-first, but here, the noun – or the subject of the expression is fronted. This is for emphasis. And the predicate – or the action/the verb that is being done to them (or shouldn't be done) is shifted to the rear of the sentence *tàire a dhèanamh orra*. So, in a sense, we're presented with the picture of the boy and the horse – and then once that is in mind, the action.

Also, note that as is often the case, Gaelic expresses an idea by what is called "nominalization" – the use of a noun rather than a verb. In this example, *scorn made on them* rather than *scorn them*. We see this in many common Gaelic expressions

- *Tha gaol agam ort* – "I have love on you" (or, "My love is on you") rather than *I love you*
- *Tha tinneas orm* – "Sickness is on me," rather than *I am sick*

Imagination vs. reality

Bidh adharcan an tairbh nas motha anns a' cheò

The horns of the bull are larger in the fog.

Which may be said of anything we can't see clearly (including the difficulties of a new language that we've just begun learning!).

There is nothing uniquely Gaelic about this observation. Indeed, it is a secret well known to filmmakers of horror movies who very often don't clearly or completely show the "monster" until later in the movie, for well they know that our imaginations construct scarier images than what we can see clearly. But this *seanfhacal* reminds us that a culture's immediate environment colors its expression of even universal truths. In this proverb, we see two things that are particular to the Highland Gaelic experience: bulls and fog!

Language Notes

Bidh adharcan – *Bidh* is the future tense of the verb "to be." As noted elsewhere, in Gaelic the future tense not only communicates future action (or state of being), but also a continual, habitual condition – an idea that in English is expressed by the simple present as you can see in the translation: contrast the English *The horns of the bull* **are** *larger* with the literal translation of the Gaelic *The horns of the bull* **will be** *larger*.

When you're down and out

Nuair a dh'fhàgadh tu casruisgte, teichidh do chàirdean bhuat.

When you are left barefoot, your friends flee from you.

Many people have enjoyed the song "Bridge over Troubled Water" that speaks of undying fidelity through times of adversity:

> When you're weary, feeling small
> When tears are in your eyes, I will dry them all, all
> I'm on your side, oh, when times get rough
> And friends just can't be found
> Like a bridge over troubled water
> I will lay me down

But such romanticism seems to be antithetical to the Gaelic sensibility, for our proverb points to a sad truth voiced by blues artist Bessie Smith in the song "Nobody knows you when you're down and out."

> Once I lived the life of a millionaire
> Spent all my money, I just did not care
> Took all my friends out for a good time
> Bought bootleg liquor, champagne and wine
> Then I began to fall so low
> Lost all my good friends, I did not have nowhere to go
> Cause no, no, nobody knows you
> When you're down and out

There are many examples we can draw upon in Scottish history and literature. Just a couple:

- Mary Queen of Scots was immensely popular when she first was crowned but fell out of favor with many Scottish nobles, who eventually abandoned her when she was imprisoned by the English Queen Elizabeth I.
- William Wallace, who spearheaded the initial resistance to English conquest in the Scottish Wars of Independence, was eventually betrayed by fellow Scots – many of whom had originally supported the cause of Scottish freedom – and was turned over to the English and subjected to the horrible execution of being hung, drawn, and quartered.

Indeed, nobody knows when you're down in London with the hangman's noose around your neck.

On inevitability

Thig Latha-Nollaig.

Christmas-day will come.

A lot of power of implication are embedded in these three simple words. Said of things that seem far off, but a reminder to us that they will eventually happen. A truth especially pertinent in a rural environment such as the traditional Gaelic culture, in which time was experienced more as cyclycal than linear: Seasons come and go and then come again. As our experience of the natural environment which surrounds us influences our mindset, this observation might also extend to human activity, as well: What has happened before will happen again – even if not exactly, as Mark Twain is reputed to have noted, "History doesn't repeat itself, but sometimes it does rhyme."

Thig Latha Nollaig.

Language Notes

Thig = the simple future of the verb thig / to come (verbal noun = a' tighinn). One of the ten irregular Gaelic verbs, it does not form the future tense according to the regular pattern, but idiosyncratically (which is why it is called "irregular").

Out of sight

An rud a thèid fad on t-sùil, thèid e fad on chridhe.

What goes far from the eye, goes far from the heart.

Somewhat like the English expression, "out of sight, out of mind." About how we tend to forget the personal meaning of what is no longer present. Only in the Gaelic expression, it is not from the mind that it goes, but much more poignantly -- much more feelingly -- from our *hearts*. Perhaps why it is important to continually keep reminders in front of us – "close to our eye" – of those people, things, and ideas that are most important to us.

Language Notes:

a thèid = "that goes" ... the relative pronoun *a* and the simple future tense – so literally, that will go. However, in Gaelic, the future tense can also communicate the habitual, the continual – in other words, that which is always true, whereas in English, this idea is communicated by the simple present tense. To get an idea how this works, contrast the English "goes" with the Gaelic "will go."

on t-sùil / **on** chridhe = "from the" – sometimes seen as *bhon*, from the root word *bho*; *bhon* is a contraction of *bho an*.

Enjoy the good while it lasts

Gabh an latha math 'fhad 's a gheibh thu e.

William McTaggart *Spring* (1864)

Take the good day while you may.

Similar to, but not quite as aggressive as the mistranslated "seize the day," which often is understood as encouraging hedonistic excess, evoking the idea of taking what you can, of being proactive and grabbing happiness, often by buying more and more stuff you can 't afford; of being constantly busy, busy, busy; of encouraging sleep deprivation as a virtue; of 'working till you drop'; or as the billboard advertisement for a health club once proclaimed, of the idea that "You can sleep when you're dead."

This bit of advice relates more to accepting what good comes your way because it might not last. It is not quite so lackadaisical as the Biblical proverb, "And why do you worry about clothes? See how the flowers of the field grow. They do not labor or spin. Yet I tell you that not even Solomon in all his splendor was dressed like one of these." (Matthew 6:28-29)

This Gaelic *seanfhacal* reflects the experience of a people who were well-used to hardships; for whom spring often comes late, and winter too early;

who lived in an environment where even summer days require sweaters and coats. (I once heard a tourist in Scotland say, "The coldest winter I ever knew was a summer day in Glencoe.") Outside the literal applications, the environment of the *Gàidhealtachd* (the "Highlands" as they are known in English) was often one of privation, poverty, and oppression. So, it makes sense that one would be advised to enjoy a good day because it may not last long.

And I wonder if there isn't something almost Zen about the proverb as well: how it tells us we should be mindful and grateful of the beauty of a day because wherever we live in whatever circumstances, the "day" will eventually pass, and if we have neglected to savor it, we may come to regret having missed it.

For me, this expression has a bit of a Zen quality to it – reminding us to live in the moment, to be aware of the moment. Many times, we let the present slip away from us because we're thinking of something else: Like the Adam Sandler character in the movie Click, who has the magical power to fast-forward his life to the 'important' stuff: work, achievement, success – only to realize that these were not important at all, and he has fast-forwarded past what was really important – the enjoyment of a day, the love of family, time he should have cherished but sped past.

Gaelic poetry and song is replete with reminders to enjoy the present day. A winning poem from a recent Gaelic Mòd encouraged the full experiencing of life, a revelation inspired by watching a dog enthusiastically frolicking in the snow:

Bu choir dhuinn a bhith	We should be
mar chuilean san ùr-sneachd	Like a puppy in new-fallen snow
a' mothachadh fìrinneachd 's gu dearbh	Sensing reality and indeed
a' faighinn fios-faireachdainn le gach nearbh	Experiencing with each nerve
a' blasadh beò ma milis no searbh	Tasting life whether sweet or bitter
a' faireachdainn aiteis àird le gach lèith	Feeling joy with each nerve
's a' bhith beò anns gach fèith.	And life in each sinew

The question might arise, how do we reconcile this proverb with those that admonish us to remember the past? Isn't remembering the past the opposite of living in the present?

Not really, I would answer. Like the mid-twentieth century American author William Faulkner once wrote, "The past is never dead. It's not even past," the past – both our personal experiences and the histories of those who have come before us continue to live on in the present in that they have shaped us into the people we are today. In a sense, if you don't know where you have come from, you can't really know where you are right now.

Sometimes our remembrance of the past provides us a second look at the moments that have flitted by and this memory reminds us that we should pay closer attention to what remains in our time now. There's another Gaelic song that speaks to us of this: "Cha Till e Tuille - Cumha Mhic Criomain" (He will not return – McCrimmon's Lament).

Cha chluinnear do cheòl san Dùn mu fheasgar	Your music will not be heard in Dunvegan this evening
'S mac-talla nam mìr le mùirn ga fhreagairt	And the echo on the ramparts mourning in answer
Gach fleasgach us àigh, gun cheòl gun bheadrach	Each young man and maiden without music or merriment
O'n thriall thu bhuainn, 's nach till thu tuilleadh	Since you have abandoned us, and you will never return

A reminder to us that we should fully enjoy each day as it comes because once gone, it will not come again.

A small spark

Is tric a lasas sradag bheag teine mòr.

It's often that a small spark kindles a large fire.

Similar to the English *mighty oaks from little acorns grow.*

Huge events often proceed from small "sparks" (both literal and figurative). Every forest fire, for instance, starts with a small spark literally. (That is, the huge forest fire doesn't suddenly begin as a large forest fire.)

In 1306, Robert the Bruce and John Comyn, the two main rivals for the crown of Scotland, met in the small Greyfriars Church, Dumfries. We don't know what sparked the fight, for the two men were meeting privately to discuss uniting their efforts in the battle against the English invaders; it could have been a minor insult or a cross word, a small "spark," indeed, but it led to Robert killing his rival, which in turn led eventually to Robert becoming King

Robert the Bruce, and the eventual ousting of the English king and army from Scotland.

In July 1745, Prince Charles Edward Stuart, along with just seven companions, first set foot on Scottish soil on the tiny island of Eriskay in the Outer Hebrides. His contingent was small, he had no arms, nor army, nor money, nor even the unequivocal loyalty and backing of the Highland clans from whom he sought support. But it was that small "spark" that started a conflagration that nearly won an empire.

It's not just war and rebellion that can be sparked. So can birth: The movement to revive Gaelic education was instigated by a succession of tiny sparks. In 1973, a Scottish businessman Sir Iain Noble donated a small plot of land and an old stone barn on the Isle of Skye to a group that began a Gaelic college; and so *Sabhal Mòr Ostaig* was born, an institution of higher education dedicated to Gaelic, which now offers both individual language classes as well as degrees in Gaelic language and Gaelic related studies, such as music, education, and the environment. And it all began with a small, humble, ancient barn.

He who accuses

Am fear a bhios ciontach fhèin, cha sguir e a thogadh casaid-bhrèige air chàch.

The person who is guilty themselves won't stop accusing others.

An observation of a trait that in modern times is known as the psychological behavior of "projection," which can be either the conscious or unconscious projecting of one's own faults or traits upon others. For instance, the liar accuses everyone else of lying. The thief thinks everybody else is out to steal from him.

In the Gaelic myth of Dèirdre -- often known as Dèirdre of the Sorrows in English; in Gaelic, *Dèirdre nam Bròn* – the young woman Dèirdre runs away with her true love Naoise rather than be forced to marry Conchobar the old King. When they are captured, in spite of her professions of love for Naoise,

Conchobar accuses Naoise of abducting the girl against her will – the same thing he was intending to do: force her into marriage with him.

A painting of Deirdre in *A book of myths* (1915), by Helen Stratton.

In many long-standing clan feuds, such as between the Campbells and the MacDonalds, both sides often accused the other of theft and murder to justify their own theft and murder.

During the 1700s and 1800s when many landowners ruthlessly evicted Highland Gaels from their homes, the powerful lords projected moral and economic faults upon the Highlanders: They were lazy, unproductive, ignorant, backward, resistant to progress. These accusations served to deflect attention from the landlords' own greed and cruelty.

Language Notes

casaid-bhrèige / *casaid* = accusation, *bhrèige* (from brèug) = lie; in other words, a "lying" (or false) accusation. Here, the phrase is *tog casaid-bhrèige air* – to lift (or make) a false accusation on (or against).

Inevitability

Ruithidh an taigeis fhèin le bruthaich.

Even a haggis runs downhill.

In line with the tendency of idioms to be constructed out of the experiences of people in a society – the social behavior, beliefs, customs, and material culture, Gaelic traditional culture was not *clock-oriented* in the way that in contemporary English-language society is and from which we have the expression, *even a broken clock is right twice a day*. That said, what are two things that were very common in the traditional Highland culture? *Haggis and hills*! And so, we have the expression of the idea that even something that is normally unlikely might yet happen. I find it very interesting how this is not a statement of an absolutist mindset, but is actually quite contemporary in a quantum-physics sort of way in that it reflects upon the *probability* of something happening however unusual or contrary to expectations of the normal order of things.

There's a deeper meaning embedded in this expression as well. For it expresses how even something that is stationary and unmoving will under the right circumstances and with the right impetus – in this case, gravity and a slope – achieve the impossible: movement!

For a long time, the minority status of the Gaelic language seemed to be an inevitable, immovable fact. However, in recent years, thanks to the impetus provided by dedicated language activists and educators, Gaelic is experiencing a resurgence in the form of the establishment of Gaelic Medium Education not only in the traditional Gàidhealtachd but in the major "Lowland" cities, as well; a college dedicated to Gaelic study and Gaelic subjects; even the worldwide spread of opportunities to learn Gaelic via the Internet.

Language Notes

Ruithidh – will run. First, the future tense of regular Gaelic verbs (all but 10 of Gaelic verbs) is formed by adding a suffix (*-aidh* or *-idh*) to the root verb.

But here, what is nominally the "future" tense is not really speaking of a future event, but of a continual, habitual occurrence, as in *The sun **rises** in the morning*.

Where the pigs are

Far am bi a' mhuc, bidh fail.

Where the pig is, that's where a pigsty will be.

Similar to the Biblical phrase, "By their fruits you shall know them," this proverb observes how a person not only influences their environment but creates it. In this instance, a pigsty doesn't just exist – waiting for the pig to come along, but rather comes into existence through the presence and working of the pig.

As with so many proverbs, the terms are to be understood metaphorically and extend beyond the literal meaning. If you travel through the Highlands today, you'll see many *tobhtaichean* (singular, *tobhta*) – ruins of cottages where there once existed thriving communities. These ruins didn't just happen to appear out of nowhere – but in many instances were the result of the actions emanating from the greed and the landlords who instigated the ethnic cleansings known as the Highland Clearances.

In the same way, the sad state of Gaelic language and culture today is the creation of the work of hundreds of years of "pigs" who worked to create a "pigsty" -- a space of ruination -- in the *Gàidhealtachd*, or in other words, a ruined village out of our heritage. It should be remembered that these are not just tumbled-down buildings. When Gaelic poets sang songs of the lost homeland, it wasn't just the loss of the cottages that they lamented, but the *dùthaich* that nurtured them – the village, the natural environment, the community.

We need to be aware that even though the proverb focuses on the negative, the opposite holds true, too. Our actions and behavior can create gardens as well as pigsties. For instance, the growing institution of Gaelic medium education – the teaching of school children through the medium of the Gaelic language – is helping to revitalize the "garden" of Gaelic language and culture.

Going further, traditional Gaelic culture was in part maintained through the informal institution of the *cèilidh* house – a place where people gathered for the sharing of the music, stories, dance, and shared affinity that fostered the cohesion of the community and the continuation of the culture. Today, we can participate in the building of a new Gaelic garden (so to speak) through the remembrance of Gaelic history, stories, songs, music, festivities.

Language Notes

Far am bi ... *Where* is ... Gaelic has two words for "where." One is used in questions, such as *Càit' a bheil fail?* (Where is a pigsty?), and the other "where" is used as here in dependent clauses – which can be seen more readily if we restructure the sentence: *Bidh fail far am bi a' mhuc* (The pigsty is *where* the pig is) or *Bidh a' mhuc far am bidh an fhail* (The pig is where the pigsty is). Notice, neither is a question.

The best sauce

'S math an t-annlann an t-acras.

Hunger is a good sauce

Nothing ever tastes so good as when you're hungry. In Robert Louis Stevenson's novel *Kidnapped*, set in the Scottish Highlands, David Balfour is shipwrecked and finds himself stranded alone on an isolated island and without resources. Desperately hungry, he finds a couple shellfish and "Of these two I made my whole diet, devouring them cold and raw as I found them; and so hungry was I, that at first they seemed to me delicious." (Shortly afterwards, he retches them up, which only emphasizes the point: Such a "good sauce" was his hunger that he didn't notice how wretched they actually were!)

Poverty and scarcity was rife and frequent in Gaelic culture: hence the recourse to the simplest ingredients in our cultural diet: *taigeis* (haggis), made from the innards of sheep and oats; *ceann cropaig*, a tasty treat of fishing communities in the Highlands, consisting of animal fat, liver, and oats boiled in a fish head (the more valuable parts of the fish having been sold). Highland cattle drovers used to make flat oatcakes and store them under the saddles of their horses, where the body heat of the animals would cook them (after a fashion). The hunger of the Highlanders made a delicious meal out of a simple horse-sweat- salted *bonnach*.

Language Notes

'S math – literally, "is good the hunger the sauce," though perhaps translated into syntactical English, might be read as "it is good" as English syntax demands a subject of a verb, even when one doesn't really exist (as in this case, what is "it"?). Anyway, here we see the assertive verb "be" that is usually used to assert identity between two things – but in this case for emphasis *asserting* that something is good. Gaelic allows for great variability in the ordering of its sentences, according to the desire of the speaker/writer to emphasize parts of the idea, or for whatever other reason; By way of comparison, other ways to phrase the idea would be

- *'S e an t-acras an t-annlann math* -- it is the hunger (that is) the good sauce.
- *'S e an t-annlann math an t-acras* – it is the good sauce (that is) the hunger
- *'S e annlann math a tha ann an acras* – it is a good sauce that is (in) hunger

annlann -- accompaniment or condiment (anything served alongside the main course)

acras – hunger. In Gaelic, you don't say, "I am hungry," but rather, *Tha an t-acras orm* – "Hunger is on me." Quite often, emotions or experiences – especially those we cannot control are *on* us, as if they have settled on us outside our will or volition.

In the shadows

An rud a bhios air a dhèanamh anns a' chùil, thig e a dh'ionnsaigh an t-solais

The thing that is done in the dark will be brought to light.

Although cùil is often translated in this context as "dark" or "darkness," it literally refers to a corner, or a niche. Perhaps, the "darkness" translation alludes to the interior of Highland cottages before electric lighting brought daylight-brightness inside at night, and all light was supplied by dim candles, so anything done in the corner of the cottage was literally in the dark. Sometimes, the proverb has the thing done in the shadows as being brought to the fire – that is, the hearth – so, brought out of the shadows in the corner of the cottage into the light in the center of the cottage.

Language Notes

air a dhèanamh – one of the ways of stating the passive voice. (Grammar lesson: active voice = He did something. Passive voice: Something was done.) In this construct, the verb bi (to be) acts as a 'helping verb' which combines with the possessive pronoun and the verbal noun. Remember that the pronoun is always gendered masculine or feminine as Gaelic has no neuter case (that is, no "it"). So, the form looks something like this:

- o ***Bha e air a dhèanamh*** – He was on his doing / It was done (the masculine possessive pronoun lenites)
- o ***Bha mi air mo bhualadh*** – I was on my hitting / I was hit (the first-person possessive pronoun lenites)
- o ***Bha i air a faicinn*** – She was on her seeing / She was seen (the feminine possessive pronoun does not lenite)

cùil – corner, niche (*anns a' chùil* – in the corner.

-

Steal a little

Am fear a ghoideadh ugh na circe, ghoideadh e ugh an geòidh.

He one who would steal the hen egg would steal the goose egg.

The "goose egg" is much larger than the egg of the hen (a chicken), so in essence what is meant by this *seanfhacal* is that a person who would commit a small crime would commit a large one.

ghoideadh – "would steal," from the verb *goid*, "to steal." One of the ways to express the conditional verb form (for regular verbs) in Gaelic is to start with the root verb, lenite it, and add either +*eadh* or +*adh* (which one, depends on whether the last vowel of the root verb is broad – that is, a, o, u – or slender – i, e (following the rule, broad-to-broad, slender-to-slender). For example:

- *goid* (to steal) > *ghoid+eadh* = *ghoideadh* (would steal)
- *seòl* (to sail) > *sheòl + adh* = *sheòladh* (would sail)

Words that begin with a vowel are "lenited" in a different way (which is not called lenition, but in some instances, it serves the same purpose). They add a dh' prefix:

- *òl* (drink) > *dh'òl+adh* = *dh'òladh*

Give two eyes to yourself

Bheir dà shùil ort fhèin mus toir thu aon sùil air neach eile.

Look at yourself with two eyes before you put one eye on somebody else.

In his poem "To a Louse" (which the reader might be more familiar with by the plural *lice*), Robert Burns describes the blood-sucking parasite which he sees crawling upon the bonnet of a woman who fancies herself "sae fine a lady" -- so far superior to having her hair infested with lice like a poor beggar. He advises "Jenny," the woman in question, that she should take a stern look at herself and issues the invocation:

> O wad some Pow'r the giftie gie us
> To see oursels as others see us!
> It wad frae monie a blunder free us

An' foolish notion.

And so, this *seanfhacal* encourages us all to take a hard look at ourselves "with two eyes" before we look squint-eyed at someone else.

The company you keep

Millidh droch-cho-luadar deagh-bheus

Bad company corrupts good character.

The rotten apple spoils the barrel. Keep company with bad people, and you'll soon be one of their number.

It could be said that during the late 1700s and 1800s, Gaelic clan chiefs whose culture traditionally mandated that they care for the hereditary lands and people of their clan were corrupted by the money-grubbing, profit-driven capitalistic "bad company" of the dominant English-language society, which lead to mass evictions of Highlanders from ancestral lands in favor of sheep farms – because sheep were more profitable than people, and money was the most important value of all. So prevalent was the imposition of this regime of sheep that the Gaels dubbed the time that it happened *Bliadhna nan Caorach* – the year of the sheep.

Examples of this maxim abound in Scottish literature:

In novelist James Hogg's *The Private Memoirs and Confessions of a Justified Sinner,* the protagonist falls under the influence of the mysterious Gil-Martin. This association leads to the corruption of his character and his committing terrible crimes. (A little sidenote: Gille-Martain is the name of a fox/trickster character in Gaelic folklore.)

In Walter Scott's *The Heart of the Midlothian*, the innocent Effie Dean becomes associated with a bad crowd, including her lover.

This association corrupts her and leads to her being falsely accused of and imprisoned for murder.

Where you come from

An luibh a dh'fhàsas às an òcraich, 's e as àirde a thogas a cheann.

The weed that grows out of the dung heap lifts her head the highest.

This proverb could be taken two ways: positively and negatively.

Positively, it could be thought to reflect the essentially democratic nature of Gaelic (& Scottish) culture, as expressed by Robert Burns (though in English):

> The honest man, tho' e'er sae poor,
> Is king o' men for a' that.

Negatively, it could be a commentary on the *just made it* -- the *nouveau riche* (the newly-rich) or the *parvenu* (the just-arrived) -- to flaunt their wealth, their status, and their power because they are so insecure that they have to let everybody know how important they are, to the point that they feel they must gold plate even their toilets.

Language Notes

A dh'fhàs / a thogas = we should recognize these as the relative independent future/habitual form

Òcraich = politely "dung" (as you will find it translated in more formal sources), but also manure, pile of excrement, or most crudely, "shit pile."

As àirde = superlative, the highest. The superlative in Gaelic is often phrased as if it were a noun (indeed, we see this tendency in some English phrasings, too, as in "***the*** highest"), and so it requires in these usages the assertive verb ***Is*** rather than ***Bi***.

Your greatest enemy

Na daoine a thug buaidh air fhèin thug iad buaidh air an nàmhaid.

Those who conquer themselves conquer their enemy.

The mid-twentieth century Gaelic poet *Somhairle MacGill-Eain* (Sorley MacLean) writes in his collection of poems *Dàin do Eimhir* (Poems to Eimhir) about his internal struggles between questions of personal fulfilment in his love for a woman (the eponymous Eimhir), and his responsibilities to the wider world.

Bàrd a' strì ri càs an t-saoghail,	A poet struggling with the world's condition,

Siùrsachd bhuadhan is an daorsa
Leis na mhealladh mòr-roinn dhaoine,

Cha mhise fear a chanadh, shaoil leam,
Gun tugadh reic an anama faochadh.

Ach thubhairt mi rium fhìn, 's cha b' aon-
    uair,
gun reicinn m' anam air do ghaol-sa

Prostitution of talents and the bondage
With which the bulk of men have been
    deceived,
I am not, I think, one who would say
That the selling of the soul would give
    respite.

But I did say to myself, and not once,
That I would sell my soul for your love

I think in this we see that the issue is not in the particular choices that we make, but that we conquer the "enemy" – our doubting selves -- and make a choice.

Necessity

'S e an èiginn a chuir am fiadh thar an locha.

Necessity made the deer swim across the loch.

Related to the English-language proverb, "necessity is the mother of invention," this *seanfhacal* tells us something a little bit different, for it doesn't speak to creating something that didn't exist before ("inventing") but rather to doing something out of the ordinary, perhaps even dangerous (perhaps akin to "desperate circumstances call for desperate measures"), certainly something out of our comfort zones (or what we would like to have remained comfortable zones).

There are many stories in Gaelic folklore about people driven by circumstances of desperate poverty to leave their homes and "seek their fortunes" in the wider world. For example, in the story *A Mhaighdeann Mhara* (The Sea Maiden), a fisherman makes a bargain with a magical being (a kind of mermaid) – successful fishing in exchange for his first-born son. It was the necessity of poverty and starvation that "sent him across that *lake* (figuratively speaking, of course). But that's not the end of the story: As the years go by, the fisherman delays and procrastinates fulfilling his end of the bargain until finally the son grows to full-size and with his father facing the necessity of finally being forced to pay what is owed the sea-maiden, the now-grown boy has a sword made and ventures out to face adventures such as fighting a giant and a beast with three heads (to finally win the hand of the princess). *Necessity made the boy swim across* **that** *lake.*

In a less fanciful way, we in the Gaelic disapora owe our people's dispursion across the globe to the necessities of poverty and oppression forced upon us in the homeland: Why so many Gaels in ages past climbed aboard ships and sailed out to the strange, wild lands of America and Australia (amongst others).

Language Notes

syntax – literally, the sentence reads, It's necessity that sent the deer across the lake.

Thar an locha – across the lake; the preposition *thar* takes the genitive noun.

What makes a table

Cha bhòrd bòrd gun aran ach 's bòrd aran leis fhèin.

**A table without bread is not a table, but bread is a table
on its own.**

"Bread" is being used metaphorically. The emphasis is on the substance of
the meal rather than on the setting. No matter how poor the surroundings, if
we have necessities enough to sustain life, that is "table" enough.

Language Notes

This is a grammatical construction that might be helpful for the learner to
examine. First, we have …

Cha bhòrd bòrd – a table is not a table. The learner might ask, where's the
verb? The verb is the assertive verb *is*; it does not appear because in

the negative, it is understood. As well, the negative (cha) lenites the noun that follows. But the second bòrd is not negated, so it is not lenited. So, what we have here is *cha bhòrd bòrd* – a table is not a table, or to follow the Gaelic syntax, is not a table a table.

's bòrd aran – bread is a table. Again, we see the assertive verb "be," which is used to assert that one thing is another thing (here, that bread **is** a table), only in this instance, the sentence does not state the negative (not a table) but the positive (is a table), so there is no lenition.

structure – in both cases, the order of the noun-elements is reversed from what it would be in English. In both of these phrases, the part that English would put first (the positive table – is a table; and bread) comes second in Gaelic, and the part that English would put second (negative table – not a table; table) comes first. So, literally, the sentence might be literally translated as

Cha	bhòrd	bòrd	gun	aran	ach	's	bòrd	aran	leis fhèin.
Not (is)	a table	a table	without	bread	but	is	a table	bread	by itself

Hope that helps!

The insight of a friend's eye

'S math an sgàthan sùil caraid.

A friend's eye is a good mirror.

Those who know us best see us the most clearly. Seemingly in opposition to the saying that "love is blind," the distinction can be explained like this: In the Gaelic framing, we see our friends clearly for we are their "mirrors." Like in the legend of Fionn and Sadhbh, we don't love them any less for their faults – for we don't expect them to be perfect -- we still love them despite their flaws.

Language Notes:

Syntax – literally, Is good the mirror of a friend's eye.

Syntax – Gaelic "packs" the nouns together in a way that creates an equivalence – "sgàthan sùil caraid" – literally, *Is good the **mirror of an eye of a friend***.

'S math -- using of the "assertive verb" (*IS*) with an adjective (*math*) emphasizes the quality of a thing, creating a statement – or an assertion -- much stronger than simply saying "Tha sùil caraid math" (An eye of a friend is good).

Quiet waters, and thin streams

Far as sàmhaiche an uisge, 's ann as doimhne e.

Far as taine an abhainn, 's ann as fuaimniche i.

Where the water is most quiet, it is there that it is deepest.

Where the river is shallowest, it is there that is the noisiest.

Similar to the English "Still waters run deep." (Which phrase is, however, oxymoronic – as *still* waters are **still**, and don't run at all!)

But that aside, another example (if we need to be reminded) of the tendency of a people (not just Gaelic people) to draw lessons and examples, metaphors and illustrations from the physical environment in which they live. And there are few things more common in the Scottish Highlands than water – and lots of it! In still lakes, in quickly running streams, and sometimes not even confined to bodies of water but encroaching upon the land and soaking the ground! So, it's not to be wondered at that Gaelic draws upon the behavior of water to illustrate a commonly observed trait.

Language Notes

This *seanfhacal* presents us with examples of the superlative (which is, put simply, the form the adjective takes when you want to say that one thing is *biggest* or *most* (or whatever, for instance). You might notice a pattern: The adjective is slenderized – an "i" is inserted in the last syllable -- and augmented with an "e," so

Adjective	English	Superlative	English
Sàmhach	Quiet	*As sàmhaiche –*	quietest
Domhainn	Deep	*As doimhne* = (note *syncope*, or contraction -- not *domhainne)	deepest
Tana	Thin, shallow	*As taine*	shallowest
Fuaimneach	Noisy	*As fuaimniche*	noisiest

If the adjective is already slender (that is, already contains an "i" as its last vowel), no further slenderization is required.

Fuaimneach is slenderized by converting the "*ea*" in the last syllable to "*i*" (not adding an "*i*" which would give us **fuaimneaiche.*

Just like in English in which some adjectives don't follow the *+est* rule (for example, the superlative of *bad* is not *baddest* but *worst*), there are a number of irregular Gaelic adjectives which don't follow this rule, but for the most part.

A little piece for the beast.

Mir am beul na bèiste.

A bite in the monster's mouth.

In some traditions, this saying is thought to refer to the story of the traveler threatened by a pack of wolves, whom he temporarily stalls by throwing out one "bite" after another for them to eat. In other words, an expedient sacrifice for temporarily staving off disaster.

In the *Gàidhealtachd*, oftentimes Fairies were appeased with small offerings lest they become angered and cause harm. John Gregorson Campbell tells the story of a human woman whose cow failed in its milk production. Investigating, she caught a Fairy woman stealing the milk of her cow. The Fairy explained that her own child was sick and asked permission to milk the cow for her child for a month. The human woman agreed to giving the "bite" to the beast, and at the end of the month, the cow was restored to the human and to full productivity. Following this story, there were customs in some parts of the Highlands of leaving small vessels of milk out in the pastures, so the fairies wouldn't steal milk from the farmers' cows.

Other examples of "bites" given to appease the beast abound.

In his book *A Description of the Western Isles of Scotland,* published in 1716, Martain Martin records the ceremony on the Isle of Lewis of the fisherfolk giving a "*mir*" of ale to a spirit of the sea, which offering they hoped would be returned to them in the form of seaweed that they depended upon to fertilize their fields. Martin wrote

> The Inhabitants of this Island had an ancient custom making a sacrifice to a Sea-God, called *Shony*, at [Halloween.] ... Every Family furnished a [quarter bushel of] Malt, and this was brewed into Ale: one of their number was picked out to wade into the Sea up to [his] middle, and carrying a Cup of Ale in his hand, standing still in that posture, cried out with a loud Voice, saying, "*Shony*, I give you this Cup of Ale, hoping that you'll be so kind as to send in plenty of [seaweed], for enriching our ground [for the coming year]; and so threw the Cup of Ale into the Sea."

Outside of folklore and in actual history, we have an example of a *mir* for the beast in the Battle of Perth in 1696. The clans Chattan and Cameron had been engaged in a long-standing feud that had spanned decades. In order to avoid further – and massive – bloodshed, King Robert II devised a *mir* to appease the "beast" of the ongoing clan war.

The King ordered a limited battle of 30 men on each side. The warriors could carry weapons – swords, axes, bows and arrows, and daggers – but armor was forbidden.

Sir Walter Scott portrayed the battle in his novel *The Fair Maid of Perth*:

> The trumpets of the king sounded a charge, the bagpipes blew up their screaming and maddening notes, and the combatants, starting forward in regular order, and increasing their pace till they came to a smart run, met together in the center of the ground, as a furious torrent encounters an advancing tide. For an instant or two the front lines, hewing at each other with their long swords, seemed engaged in a succession of single combats; but the second and third ranks soon came up on either side, actuated alike by the eagerness of hatred and the thirst of honor, pressed through the intervals, and rendered the scene a tumultuous chaos, over which the huge swords rose and sunk, some still glittering, others streaming with blood ...

There are various accounts of the outcome of the combat – some giving the survivors as one warrior on one side and 11 on the other, while another account gives the survivors as five and two.

In any event, the "beast" was satisfied with this little "piece" of a battle, and a larger clan war had been averted.

Fate

Am fear don dàn a chrochas, cha tèid gu brath a bhàthadh.

The man who is fated to hang will not drown.

This *seanfhacal* does not express a Gaelic belief in pre-destination or "fate," per se – that is an outcome pre-determined, but is more similar to the observation of the ancient Greeks, who held that "character is fate."

There has long been a belief in Gaelic culture of the efficacy of seers – people with druidical powers to see what is to come. The Scottish poet Thomas Campbell, who was of Highland descent though he wrote in English, wrote of "Lochiel's Warning": In the poem, Cameron of Lochiel, the chief of Clan Cameron, is warned by a "Wizard" of the disaster that will befall the Highland clans at Culloden:

Lochiel! Lochiel, beware of the day
When the Lowlands shall meet thee in battle array!
For a field of the dead rushes red on my sight,
And the clans of Culloden are scattered in fight:
They rally, they bleed, for their kingdom and crown;
Woe, woe to the riders that trample them down!
Proud Cumberland prances, insulting the slain,
And their hoof-beaten bosoms are trod to the plain.

Coinneach Odhar, "The Brahan Seer," is famous in Highland legend for having possessed *an dà shealladh* – the "second sight" (though, actually, the Gaelic phrase is correctly translated as "the two sights). He is reputed to have foretold the disaster of Culloden Moor, the "black rain" that would bring riches to the North East of Scotland (the North Sea oil), and the "sheep that would eat men" (the ethnic cleansing of the Highlands in favor of sheep farms), but the most fateful prophecy he ever told was pronounced when the wife of the chief of his clan (the MacKenzies of Seaforth) demanded that he tell her what her husband was doing on his long journey away from home. At first, the seer demurred, but when pressed (and threatened), he told her he saw her husband with another woman, one who was more beautiful than she was and whom he loved more than he loved her. The wife didn't like his vision (which was actually true) and ordered him executed. Before he was put to death, the Seer uttered his last prophecy – one about the demise of the Seaforth family in stunning detail – that the last in the line would be deaf and dumb (which, again, turned out to be true.

In this sense, "fate" does not mean that such-and-such a thing is forced to happen, but more like it is *seen* as happening – almost as if the future and the present co-exist, and that the future is seen – much like in contemporary popular fiction, as another dimension. (Though often, the "sight" is indistinct and ambiguous – perhaps, something like a dream whose import is not clearly understood.)

It's odd that a proverb about he who is fated to hang should take this turn, but that's where the path leads us. For ideas about fate do not exist in and of themselves but co-exist with many other beliefs. While many Christian European cultures in ancient times regarded phenomena like second sight evil or satanic, such was not the case in Gaelic culture, which could be fervently Christian and at the same time hold beliefs in such things as fairies and second sight. During the infamous witch-hunts (and executions) of the 17th and 18th centuries, it was in the Scottish Lowlands (that is, the English-speaking areas) and in trading towns settled by English merchants that witches were tried and executed. Very few such persecutions were recorded in Gaelic areas. Gaels being quite comfortable with the existence of supernatural beings and the "other world," the witch-burning fervor never took hold in Gaelic territories.

There are two aspects of this second sight which bear mentioning: The first is that it is not usually regarded as a gift, sometimes more a curse. (Imagine if you were regularly haunted by the apparition of dead relatives or those about to die.) The second is that it is not controllable: Those who possess it can't just summon up a vision as if they were turning on a television or a computer screen; they'll be going about their day, and all of a sudden there's long-dead Aunt Matilda sitting at the dinner table with them!

Neither is this belief (if that 's the right word) in *an dà shealladh* a superstition of ancient Gaels only in times long past. I've encountered Gaelic people living in our present time who profess belief (though very often only with people they know and trust as the contemporary age doesn't give much credence to such things), and in some cases, people in the wider Gaelic diaspora whose ancestors emigrated from the *dùthaich* generations ago.

Recently, the Gaelic author Elidh Watts dedicated an entire book, *Gun Fhois* ("Without Peace") to her own experiences of second sight, some of them more startling than others. One story in particular that she tells illustrates both her belief in the validity of the phenomenon and its unreliabilty. She recounts a premonition of the death of her son in an accident. So real was the vision that she resolved to shelter him from the circumstances that she had foreseen and put many restrictions on his activities so that he would not suffer the fate her vision had predicted – only to have her *other* son die in the same way her revelation had foretold: You see, the vision was inexact and ambiguous, perhaps like a vaguely remembered dream, inexact, a bit blurry.

Concealing evil

Chan eil cleith air an olc ach gun a dhèanamh.

There is no concealment of evil but not to do it.

There are elements of Gaelic folk culture that are enimently practical. As you may have noticed, in these pages, there's not a lot of discussion of "good and evil, per se, as abract ultimate values, but as here, we find the very practical admonition – *You won't get away with it, so just don't do it.*

While the proverb focuses on the inevitability of discovery, it doesn't stop there. First, is the consideration of the inevitability of discovery. Second, the need to conceal the evil often entails the creation of more and more convoluted lies. And beyond concealment is the consideration of the wear and tear the evil deed inflicts on the perpetrator.

In February 1692, a detachment of British government troops were ordered to Glencoe, where they sought hospitality from the MacDonalds who lived there.

There had been some issue with the chief of the Clan MacDonald who had failed to swear allegiance to the the king before the deadline given by the government. Although the chief had attempted to pledge his loyalty, he had mistaken the location for the pledge to be given, and thus even though he had eventually done so, he had been late.

The government troops were largely men of Clan Campbell led by Captain Robert Campbell of Glen Lyon. The two clans had been enemies in a feud going back hundreds of years. This long-standing enmity did not prevent many of the people knowing each other. In fact, Captain Campbell was a friend of the leader of the small branch of MacDonalds.

The MacDonalds gave hospitality to the visiting troops for two weeks before the mass murder took place in the early morning hours of February 13th. Thirty-eighty MacDonalds were killed, some of them as they attempted to flee up the steep mountain sides that surrounded the glen. Uncounted more perished in the freezing cold.

The Massacre of Glencoe, James Hamilton

Many more might have been killed except they had been warned by the Campbell soldiers who were no doubt ashamed of what they had been ordered to do.

While the government attempted to keep the massacre secret, it was unsuccessful, in part because Captain Campbell, driven by guilt, was unable to keep silent and leaked information about the shameful evil deed.

Which illustrates the truth of the *seanfhacal*: *Chan eil cleith air an Olc ach gun a dhèanamh.*

The impossible

Chan eil air an loch nach gabh traoghadh ach fhàgail far a bheil e.

The lake that can't be drained, leave it as it is.

The legend of the Selkie might illustrate the caution contained in this maxim. The Selkie, or *maighdeann-mara* – maiden of the sea -- is a shape-shifting creature who lives in the ocean as a seal, but who is able to shed her seal-skin and come ashore as a human, either to visit or to live. When she wishes to return to the sea, she re-dons her sealskin.

There are several stories told about the *maighdeann-mara*; one of the themes that recurs is that of a young man who falls in love with the human form of such a creature and steals her sealskin and thus captures her and forces her to marry him. They have children, and are apparently happy, but in the end, she finds where he has hidden her sealskin and returns to the sea.

You see, he has attempted the impossible: attempted to drain the bottomless lake.

Language Notes

Note the Gaelic typical double-negative syntax, reflected in a somewhat literal translation: *There is **not** for the lake that **can't** be drained but leaving it where it is.* In a much more common English-language phrasing, we might say, *There is not anything that can be done with the lake that can't be drained but to leave it where it is.)*

Speaking of oars

Cha d' fhuair droch ràmhaiche ràmh math riamh.

A bad oarsman never found a good oar.

Along the lines of "a poor workman always blames his tools." We've all known people like this – people who refuse to admit their deficiencies and blame the utensils they're wielding rather than take responsibility themselves: the golfer who breaks his golf clubs because it's their fault he lost; the bad cook who blames her pots because they burnt the dinner; the musician who smashes his guitar because it played out of tune. Here, the universal observation is cast into the material-culture experience of the Highland Gael.

Language Notes

cha d' fhuair: from the verb *faigh*, one of the (few) irregular Gaelic verbs, a bit flexible in its application in that it can be translated as "get" or "find" or "reach" or "undergo" (or a number of other English words).

riamh: never, never-ever. Adds the emphatic to the "regular" negative, *cha* – that is elevates the negative verb *cha d' fhuair* from *didn't find* to *never found*.

there's no such thing as an ill wind

Cha do shèid gaoth riamh nach robh a' lìonadh an t-seòl feareigin.

A wind never blew that didn't fill somebody's sail.

notes

Like many other *seanfhaclan* (proverbs), this one not only expresses a general observation and experience, but also the material culture from which it derives. In this case, the maritime culture of the Western seaboard and the Islands of the Gaels.

Love, Gaelic style

Whether you want it or not

Thig trì nithean gun iarraidh:

an t-eagal, an t-eud, 's an gaol.

Three things come without wanting them: fear, jealousy, and love.

The rules of Gaelic grammar enforce this observation, for in Gaelic usage, these emotions are more often than not expressed as "things" that are *upon* somebody – almost as if they had settled upon the person quite outside that person's volition -- rather than emotions that somebody feels (often, as if on purpose). So, we'd say, *tha an t-eagal orm* – fear is **on me** – rather than, as in English, *I am afraid*.

This belief is reflected in numerous Gaelic tales in which love settles upon people without their wanting them, against their volition, and indeed, even against their interests.

In the classic tale of *Dèirdre* – often known as *Deirdre of the Sorrows* -- it was prophesized before her birth that she would grow to be the most beautiful woman in all of Ireland and that she would be the cause of much bloodshed and sorrow. King Conchobar was urged to kill the baby to avert the prophecy's coming to pass, but instead, he claimed her for his own and sent her away to be brought up in an out-of-the-way cottage that was isolated from all other people – and especially all other men -- until she "came of age" (that is, until the age when he could take her in marriage). However, she encounters the young hunter Naos, and they fall in love (a phrase that we have in English that, when you think about it, connotes a happenstance outside of *wanting)*. We don't have space to tell the whole story here, but suffice it to say that the King does not take kindly to his intentions for the young woman being thwarted (in a sense, to his property interests in the young woman being violated), and the love affair ends tragically.

Though not before a brief, happy sojourn in a refuge on the shores of Loch Etive in the Highlands of Scotland (and home of *the Clann Mac an t-Saoir,* I might add). A famous poem *"Dàn Chloinn Uisneachain"* – Poem of the Children of Uisneach (referring to Naos and his brothers who flee, along with Deirdre, to Scotland in order to escape the wrath of the King). The group of refugees decides to return to Ireland upon the promise of safety and protection from the King (which promise he breaks). Upon leaving, Deirdre looks back:

> Lovely land is that eastern land,
> Scotland with all its lakes.
> O! that I might not leave it!
> But I depart with Naos ...
>
> O, vale of Etive!
> where first a house was built for me.
> Delightful were its groves,
> when the sun risen to his height
> would strike his beams on Glen Etive.

The original of this version was printed in the 1805 *Report of the Highland Society on the Poems of Ossian,* in Gaelic (the English translation above), but it is a Gaelic so ancient, that I don't reprint it here. The original written version is dated to 1238 CE and was composed and found in Scotland. As an aside, we can reflect on the *pan-Gaelic* nature of the legend – on its continuance in all areas of the Gaelic world, and indeed on the sweep of its story as it encompasses the travels of its characters from Gaelic Ireland to Gaelic Scotland and back again.

As with all stories, there are many different aspects, different facets, to the events depicted, and different people can draw different "lessons" or "morals" from them. But to return to the theme of the proverb, one point we might draw from the story is that this love between Deirdre and Naos was neither wanted nor sought – indeed, if they had had a choice in the matter, they very well might have chosen differently – but it came upon them anyway, as did their sad fate.

Doubt and love

An doras air an tig amharas a-steach, thèid gràdh a-mach.

At the door where suspicion enters, love goes out

The tale of *Lasair Gheug, Nighean Rìgh Eirinn* – ("Flaming Branch," Daughter of the King of Ireland) illustrates this proverb. There was a king whose wife died and married a second wife. The second wife hated the daughter of the first and wanted to kill the girl, but couldn't for fear of the father's love. Then, she devised a plot to blame the daughter for a number of evil deeds, including killing the King's hunting dog, his prize stallion, and then even the King's son by his second wife. (Talk about an evil stepmother – she hated the daughter of the first wife so much that she killed her own child.)

The king finally lost his love for his daughter and consented to having her put to death.

SPOILER ALERT: Instead of killing the girl, the King sends her away, and she marries a magical Prince, and eventually returns to expose the evil scheming of the second Queen.

Language Notes:

An doras *air an* tig – the "air an" performs the function of a compound relative preposition, that is, "through which …" This is formed by combining the preposition with the question form of the verb – in this case, *an tig,* as in *An tig amharas a-steach air an doras? –* Does suspicion come in through the door?

Thèid – note the future tense being used as the habitual

Birds of a feather

Is beag an t-ioghnadh amadan a bhi na leannanachd ri òinsich.

It's no surprise when a fool pairs up with an idiot.

Some might think this is a cynical observation, but we have to keep in mind that more people die taking selfies than from shark attacks. The following story might illustrate an aspect of the proverb:

A cab driver came across a 21-year-old couple lying naked and severely injured on the road shortly before sunrise. Unfortunately, both individuals succumbed to their injuries at the hospital without regaining consciousness, so they were unable to tell what had happened. The circumstances remained mysterious, as there were no witnesses, no wrecked vehicles, and no sign of their clothing.

The mystery was clarified when police discovered two sets of neatly folded clothes on the roof of a nearby building. The building's roof was steep and pyramid-shaped, made of metal that was slippery from a recent rain. Police deduced that the couple had been involved in an intimate encounter on the roof, and swept up in the passion of the moment, they had lost cognizance of their precarious position and slid off to their deaths. Ironically, one of the victims bore the last name "Tumbleston," adding a final tragic irony to the story and a reminder of the truth of the Gaelic *seanfhacal.*

Language Notes:

Amadan / òinseach: Gaelic differentiates between male and female fools: "*amadan*" is most often used to refer to a male, while "*òinseach*" refers exclusively to females.

Leannanachd: to be "courting," to be "boyfriend/girlfriend." Related to the word leannan – a "lover" or "beloved" person, a "boyfriend or girlfriend."

Is beag an t-ioghnadh: *Is little the surprise,* in other words, "it's not surprising."

The nature of love

Ceilidh gràdh gràin

Love hides ugliness.

Similar to the English "Love is blind," though of course, what we're referring to here is not only physical ugliness, but flaws of all different sorts. None of us is perfect, yet our friends and partners love us (we hope) in spite of our imperfections or quirky habits.

What could better exemplify the truth of this proverb than the Gaelic love story of *Fionn Mac Cumhail* and *Sadhbh*? This is a "beauty-and-the-beast" story with a tragic twist.

Fionn (Finn in English) was the leader of the *Fianna* – the band of warrior-protectors of ancient Gaelic Ireland. He was out hunting one day and came across a deer he was about to kill, when he realized that the creature was not a deer but rather a beautiful woman – *Sadhbh* -- who had been bewitched by an evil Druid magician because she had refused to marry him.

But the curse was lifted, and she retained her human form as long as she stayed within the precincts of the territory of the Fianna.

The two fell in love, but one day Fionn had to go away. Sadhbh longed for him every day would look for his return. Finally, she thought she saw him coming home and rushed out to meet him. However, what she had seen was really the evil Druid who'd shapeshifted himself into the form of her beloved to lure her away from the safety of Fionn's land. She was turned back into a deer and ran away into the woods, but Fionn did not lose his love for her despite her beastly appearance and searched for her in the forest forever after.

Here, the point seems to be not that Fionn failed to see Sadhbh as she was, but rather that in spite of how she was, he still loved her.

Language Notes:

Ceilidh – future tense of the verb ceil (hides, conceals). As we have seen before, the continual/habitual sense is communicated using the future tense of the verb. Not to be confused with *cèilidh* (a visit).

gràdh – love

Gràin – here translated as "ugliness" – can also means deformity, or abhorrence, or something abhorrent.

Alliteration – This is a poetic technique of repeating the consonants in a series of words, as in Edgar Alan Poe's poem "Bells":

> Hear the **s**ledges with the bells—
>> **S**ilver bells!
> What a world of **m**erriment their **m**elody foretells!
>> How they **t**inkle, **t**inkle, **t**inkle,

We might take a moment to admire the "poetic" quality of the expression, something which is quite common not only in Gaelic poetry but also proverbs and even prose. Here, the hard *c* & *g* sounds, called gutturals:

Ceilidh gràdh gràin

Love of sailors

Cho teth ri gaol seòladair.

As hot as a sailor's love.

An alternative to this is sometimes "*gaol tàilleir*"— a tailor's love. Both sailors and tailors are accused of being apt to change their affections easily, probably because both traveled frequently and rarely stayed in one place for very long, and probably, too, because sailing was a frequent fact of life and livelihood amongst the Gaels on the West coast of Scotland.

There are many Gaelic songs about girls longing for their beloved sailor to return. One of the most famous is Fear a' Bhàta – The Boatman. Each day, the girl goes to the cliff overlooking the sea and peers out in hopes of seeing her beloved sailor returning to her.

'S tric mi sealltainn on chnoc as àirde	I often look from the highest hill
Dh'fheuch am faic mi fear a' bhàta	That I might see my boatman
An tig thu 'n-diugh na 'n tig thu màireach	Will you come tonight, or tomorrow?
'S mar tig thu idir gur truagh a ta mi	Oh sorry will I be if you do not come at all
Tha mo chridhe-sa briste brùite	My heart is broken, bruised
'S tric na deòir a ruith o m' shùilean	Often tears are running down from my eyes
An tig thu nochd na 'm bi mo dhùil riut	Will you come tonight, or will I wait up for you?
Na 'n dùin mi 'n doras le osna thùrsaich?	Or close the door with a sad sigh?

(I'm not aware of any such songs about a girl looking down the road for the return of a beloved tailor.)

But beyond the literal meaning, we can extend the application of this proverb to refer to anything which is powerful but ephemeral.

For example, the celebration of Hogmanay is an intense but short-lived New Year's festivity, marked by fireworks and much *hòro-gheallaidh* (hullaballoo), only to subside after a night.

In the 1690s, during the age of European exploration and colonization, the people of Scotland were overwhelmed with the passion to claim a colony in Darien Peninsula on the isthmus of Panama, which gave the venture its name of the Darien Scheme. Great sums of money were raised in Scotland to finance the venture, so great that practically all of Scotland – from common folk to lairds – had invested their life savings. However, the colony proved a failure, the venture went bust, the entire Kingdom of Scotland went broke, and the massive financial failure of the Scheme contributed to the Scottish Parliament's being forced to agree to the Union with England just a few years later.

Of love, honey, and bees

Tha am pòsadh coltach ris an t-seillean:

tha gath ann, ach tha mòran mil ann cuideachd!

Marriage is like a bee. There's a sting in it. But there's a lot of honey in it too!

The proverb speaks to the dual nature of love and marriage, capturing both its challenges and rewards. In the Gaelic experience, the "sting" is more likely than not to come from outside the relationship than from within. There are many songs and stories in which the challenges – the "stings" – suffered by the person have to do not with difficulties with the loved one, but with the circumstances surrounding the couple.

When I teach Gaelic, I often incorporate traditional songs into our lessons. My students have a running joke: They pretend surprise when we come across a "happy" Gaelic love song! There is a video skit on Youtube.com about Gaelic karaoke. Three young women (Gaelic, of course) are out for a fun night of drinks and karaoke singing. Their range of song selections run the gamut from songs about loss in war, about loss in love, to about loss in love in war.

Love makes us vulnerable, not vulnerable in the Gaelic view to the person we love, but vulnerable in the sense that their pain becomes our pain; their loss becomes our loss; and in a sense these pains are all the more acute because they come from a source we cannot control. I am vulnerable because I give myself over to you, and in that, I have no control. I can endure my own pain, but if my beloved is hurt, there's nothing I can do except suffer without remedy.

Perhaps nothing is so painful as to be separated from a loved one. Song after song in the Gaelic repertoire, for instance, dwells on the pain of separation – in the early modern period, frequently due to one person – usually the man – being away at sea. The song *"Tha mo Ghaol air àird a' Chuan"* (My Love is on the High Seas) speaks to this phenomenon of separation.

Feasgar ciùin an tùs a' Chèitein	On a quiet evening at the beginning of May
Nuair bha 'n ialtag anns na speuran	When the bat was in the skies
Chualaim rìbhinn òg 's i deurach	I heard a tearful young maiden
'Seinn fo sgàil nan geugan uain'	Singing under the shadow of the green branches
Bha a' ghrian 'sa chuan gu sèoladh	The sun was setting in the sea
'S reult cha d' èirich anns an iarmailt	And no stars yet graced the sky
Nuair a sheinn an òigh gu cianail	When the young girl sang sorrowfully
"Tha mo ghaol air àird a' chuain"	"My love is on the high seas"

In the song *"Fear a' Bhàta"* (The Boatman, or the Boat Captain), the singer recounts going to a vista point overlooking the ocean trying to see her loved "boatman" returning. In the song, she utters one of the most poignant lines in Scottish traditional songs:

*Tha mo chridhe-sa **briste brùite*** – My heart is broken and bruised

With the alliterative double "b" of ***briste brùite*** beautifully emphasizes the pangs of longing.

Robert Burns, writing in Scots, a dialect of English, writes of the ultimate separation from his beloved – that of death – in his poem "Highland Mary":

> Wi' mony a vow, and lock'd embrace,
> Our parting was fu' tender;
> And pledging aft to meet again,
> We tore oursels asunder:

> But Oh! fell Death's untimely frost,
> > That nipped my Flower sae early!
> Now green's the sod, and cauld's the clay,
> > That wraps my Highland Mary!

Not to make too much of a point of it (but that is the point, isn't it – to make the point!), here we have the expression of the "honey" of love and the "sting" that comes with it sometimes.

Language Notes:

Coltach ri = like, similar to

Tha gath **ann** = there is a sting **in it**. The use of **ann** works the same as the expletive construction in English – *there is.* Contrast these two sentences, one with ***ann*** and one without*:*

- Tha duine **ann** aig an doras = ***There is*** a man at the door
- Tha duine aig an doras. – A man is at the door.

Wit

Not if I see you first

Chì thu Hiort tro tholl do thòin mum faic thu a-rithist mi.

**You'll see St. Kilda through a hole in your ass
before you see me again.**

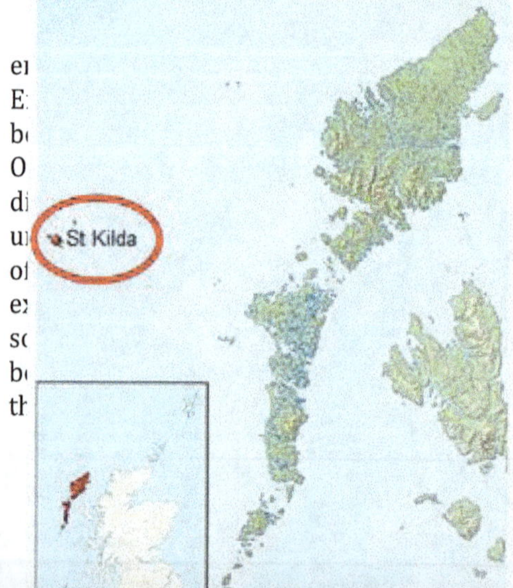

rom the social, material, and
ot surprising that Hiort, known in
phor for an inaccessible, never-to-
ed about 40 miles west of the
s (and is) accessible only with
by very infrequent ship visits
tem was comprised, quite literally,
l setting them adrift in the
ashed ashore somewhere where
s remoteness, it is thought to have
ong other things, it was famous for
p and down its high sea-cliffs to

harvest the eggs of the sea birds which nested there. It now serves as a wildlife refuge.

Hiort / St. Kilda – way out in the Atlantic, away from the mainland, or, *an tìr mhòr*, as it is called in Gaelic

Aren't you the lucky one!

Nach do rug do chat an cuilean!

Hasn't your cat given birth to a puppy!

Seanfhaclan – old sayings, proverbs – give us insight into the culture, values, and experiences of a people. In this saying, we see the value that a sheep- and cattle-herding culture places upon dogs.

In other words, you should be so lucky that your cat gives birth to valuable herding dogs!

Wise fools

'S minig a thig comhairle ghlic à bheul an amadain.

Often wise advice comes from the mouth of a fool.

Many readers are familiar with the popular film *Forest Gump,* which tells the story the "wise fool" who dispenses wisdom on his journeys and spreads happiness, kindness, and love to everyone he encounters. Such a character often appears in folk literature – two of the most prevalent examples being the child in the Hans Christian Anderson story "The Emperor's New Clothes" and another being the Fool in Shakespeare's King Lear. In both, it is the child – or the "fool" – who sees truths that other, supposedly wiser people do not.

In Gaelic tradition, the "fool" often appears as the youngest child who succeeds where their older, more accomplished siblings do not. Such is the case, for instance, in the stories of *"An Nighean 's an Duine Marbh"* (The Daughter and the Dead Man) and likewise in the story "Maol a Chliobain three sisters go off to "seek their forture." The mother offers each one of them the choice of a "big bannock and a curse" or a "small bannock and a blessing." The two older sisters, being "smarter," chose the bigger one; but out in the world, their selfishness works against them as they fail to recruit help in their struggles against the wizard who entraps them. However, the youngest sister chooses the smaller bannock and the blessing that goes along with it, and in her quest, her generosity is displayed again and again as the little creatures she shares her food with them in turn help her, and she succeeds where her older "smarter" sisters failed. The youngest girl's foolish generosity turned out to be wise, afterall.

The story "The Three Feathers" collected by Bruford and Macdonald in their book *Scottish Traditional Tales* relates how Jack, the youngest, least accomplished, and supposedly the most foolish of three sons – in fact, he's mocked by his brothers for being "daft" -- helps a frog in distress, and in return, the frog helps Jack achieve the quest his father had set for him and his brothers.

Occupational hazards

Droch thaigh aig teaghlach saoir.

A bad house of a carpenter's family.

Perhaps a universal observation, such as "the busman's holiday" (not going anywhere on vacation), or "the shoemaker's children have no shoes."

The Gaelic Crisis in the Vernacular Community, a recent study of intergenerational transmission of Gaelic – that is, of parents passing the language down to their children – found a decreasing number of children who speak Gaelic in what might be assumed to be the most Gaelic areas of the Gàidhealtachd, even in homes where parents and/or grandparents have acquired their skill, talent, and fluency in Gaelic *on ghlùin* – from their own mothers' knees. Somewhat in confirmation of the findings of the authors of the study, I myself have spoken to Gaelic speakers who are opposed to Gaelic education in the schools – saying Gaelic should be learned at home -- yet don't speak Gaelic in their homes to their own children.

I experienced this in my own family. My grandparents refused to speak Gaelic to their own children. There were, of course, practical reasons for doing this: the fact that there were relatively few employment opportunities for people who weren't fluent in English; the stigma attached to our heritage language; the hostility and bigotry directed towards Gaelic speakers – I've heard Gaels spoken of as "*teuchters*," an epithet analogous to the "n-word"; and generally speaking, the hostility that English language-culture has towards other languages -- I've seen people assaulted in public areas for speaking a language other than English (the linguist Josuah Fishman has referred to English as a "killer language").

But we have such a treasure – of language, culture, history, and literature. It's a shame not to preserve it and continue it. My long-time Gaelic tutor, Donald Mcdonald of Montreal and before that of the Isle of Harris in Scotland, believed every Gaelic speaker should be a teacher of Gaelic. Unfortunately, such is not the case. While many Gaelic speakers are happy enough to hear learners speaking the language, I have encountered a not insignificant number who seem to take the attitude that *it's not my job to teach you Gaelic,* and object to being *harassed* (as they seem to regard it) by learners trying out their new language skills. An unfortunate number of Gaelic speakers even seem to mock learners who speak Gaelic imperfectly.

Droch thaigh aig teaghlach saoir, indeed.

Language Notes

droch = "bad"; one of the few Gaelic adjectives that precedes the noun it's modifying. Like all such adjectives, it lenites the noun that follows (with a few exceptions).

<u>aig</u> teaghlach – One of the ways that Gaelic denotes possession is through the use of the preposition "aig," which even though it's often literally translated as "at," creates in this usage a (prepositional) phrase somewhat similar to the English-language *of* -- phrase, as translated here. (Compare with such phrases as *a friend of my brother, the home of my family,* etc.)

The never-ending quest

A chuir a ruith na cuthaig.

Being sent to chase the cuckoo.

A humorous expression of the worthlessness of a particular task: *being sent on a wild-goose chase*. Something like many tourists might experience who set out to track down and discover the Loch Ness Monster, the ever-elusive mythical each-uisge (water-horse) said to inhabit the depts of Loch Ness.

Or, the quest for the lost treasure of *Loch Airceig* (Loch Arkaig in English) – also called the Jacobite Gold: Said to be a cache of gold sent from Spain to finance Bonnie Prince Charlie's 1745 quest to reclaim the British crown for the House of Stuart. It arrived too late to help in the Prince's efforts, and was long thought to be secreted in the vicinity of the lake in the West Highlands. Parts of it were reputed to have been pilfered, parts were recovered, but the main body of the treasure have never been located, but hopeful treasure hunters still persist!

Language Notes

cuir: a flexible verb. Can be used for *put, plant, or send*, and like the verb "put" in English can be combined with various prepositions to form phrasal verbs in a multitude of ways such as "put up with," "put out," "put in," "put away," "put aside," and etc., so can *cuir* be modified. A few examples:

- *cuir a-mach*: throw up (lit., to put out)
- *cuir a chadal:* lull to sleep (lit., to put to sleep)
- *cuir cais air*: to annoy (lit., to put an annoyance on)
- *cuir sìos air*: translate (lit., to put down, as to put down on paper)
- *cuir clisgeadh air*: startle (lit., to put a startle on)
- *cuir daorach air*: make drunk (lit., to put a drunkenness on)
- *cuir dìmeas air*: hold in contempt, despise (lit., to put contempt on)
  - and so on and so forth, but you get the idea

ruith: can be used not only as an intransitive verb as "run" (as in "run in a race") but also as meaning 'to chase' (as here)

Where babies come from

"Càit' an d'fhuair sibh an leanabh?"

"San allt, a laochain."

**Where did you get the baby?
In the stream, little one.**

Kind of the equivalent to *the stork brought it*. We can note that folkloric expressions arise out of the circumstances and experiences of the people, their history and culture. As such, storks not being common in Scotland, Gaelic culture would have had to look elsewhere for a cute or humorous (at least, to adults) explanation of the facts of life.

But there's something else at play here. First, streams and coursing water being common in the Scottish Highlands, it might be expected that Gaels look to those as a source of babies – but especially in light of the frequent occurrence of bodies of water in Gaelic mythology and folklore. In pre-Christian (even pre-Gaelic) times, the Goddess Danu was held to be a source of life. In fact, the people who inhabited the land before the coming of the Gaels were called *Tuatha de Dana* ... People of Danu, or the Goddess Danu, who was recognized as important throughout Europe, not just Scotland, by the attachment of her name to numerous rivers such as the Don in Russia, the Danube in Central Europe, and the Dee in Scotland.

Folkloric stories abound of water spirits in Gaelic mythology: the *each-uisge*, the water horse; the *maighdeann-ròin* or seal-woman, also known as the selkie; the mysterious *Shony* of the Outer Isles, to whom the Gaels made offerings for good harvesting from the sea. Water, especially running water, was held to have magical properties – evil spirits and ghosts could not cross a flowing stream (though the water was no barrier to fairies, which might prove to be useful knowledge if you're ever chased by a supernatural being).

Language Notes

laochain – literally, "little hero," quite often applied as a term of affection to small boys, which offers us quite a bit to unpack:

- The root word *laoch* means "hero."
- Adding **-an** to the end of the word creates a diminutive, a word that would be applied something small or very young, as is sometimes done in English by adding a **-y**, as in *puppy*, or *kitty*, or **-ette** as in *kitchenette*, or **-ling**, as in *duckling*.
- Additionally, the insertion of an *i* in the last syllable marks the word laochain as being in the vocative case – that is, the mother is speaking to and addressing the "little hero." Otherwise, the word would be laochan (without the *i* insertion).

A horse and water

Bheir aon fhear each gu uisge, ach cha toir a dhà-dheug air òl.

One man may lead a horse to water, but 12 cannot make it drink.

The reader will recognize this as similar to the English-language expression of "You can lead a horse to water, but you can't make it drink," but with a difference of emphasis: **No** number of people, **no** amount of effort can make the horse drink if it doesn't want to!

There's an entertaining Gaelic folktale titled "Mac Iain Dìreach" recounted in I.F. Campbell's West Highland Tales (sometimes refashioned into English as "The Prince, the Fox, and the Sword of Light"). In the story, the hero (the *Mac Iain Dìreach* of the title) is advised by his mentor, a magical fox, how to achieve his quest and thus throw off the spell of his evil stepmother. Time and time again, the hero fails to "drink the water" of his mentor's advice – much to the amusement of the fox.

Language Notes

thoir air (*cha toir a dhà-dheug air òl)* – to make somebody do something. There's no direct translation for this expression, at least, none that makes sense in English, as literally it means something like to "take" or "give" on.

- She made Seumas leave. Literally:

Thug	i	air	Seumas	falbh
took/gave	she	on	Seumas	leaving

On getting it

"Tha biadh 's ceòl 'an seo," thuirt am madadh-ruadh, 's e a' ruith air falbh leis a' phiob.

"There's meat and music here," the fox said, when he ran away with the bagpipe.

The "sense" of the proverb might not be readily apparent, but we can unpack it a bit. It's a commonplace that the bagpipes are the honored musical centrepiece of Gaelic culture, but what is not as well known is that even in Scotland and amongst Gaels, the pipes have long been subjected to ridicule.

They are reputed to have been the favorite instrument of Satan himself. Robert Burns wrote in his poem "Tam O' Shanter,"

> A winnock-bunker in the east,
> There sat auld Nick, in shape o' beast;
> A towzie tyke, black, grim, and large,
> To gie them music was his charge:
> He screw'd the pipes and gart them skirl,
> Till roof and rafters a' did dirl.—

This linking of Satan with the bagpipes might go back to very ancient days. The god Pan of the ancient Romans – often identified as Satan in Christian mythology -- was frequently depicted as playing on the "pan-pipes," a precursor to the bagpipes. In 1679, some women were burned for sorcery; one of the accusations against them was "meeting with Satan and other witches ... where they all danced and the Devil acted as piper." In Glasgow in 1700, "a citizen one morning threw the whole town into a state of inexpressible horror and consternation by giving out that in passing at midnight through the kiryard, he saw a neighbor of his own, lately buried, rise out of the ground and dance a jig with the devil, who played [a tune] on the bagpipe."

Although in the Lowlands, the pipes were often associated with the Satanic, in the *Gàidhealtachd*, the bagpipes and the gift of piping has long been associated with the fairyfolk. Bagpipe tunes were said to be heard emanating from fairy hillocks. Manson writes that "there seems to have been the idea that pipers were the special favorites of the little harmless green-coated ones" and notes numerous stories in which Highlanders made some sort of bargain with the fairies for the gift of "singing" the pipes. (Gaelic allows for the word for "to sing" – *seinn* – and "to play" – *cluich* – both to be used in reference to the bagpipes.)

Even in the Highlands there seems to have been a tendency to joke at the expense of the pipes. To return to this well-known proverb, it is said to have originated with the story of a fox being hungry, who found a bagpipe, and proceeded to eat the bag, which of course was traditionally made of sheepskin. There was still a remnant of breath in it, and when the fox bit it the drone gave a squeal. The fox was surprised, but not frightened, hence the expression of his satisfaction. (So, the joke's on the fox, you see, who was ignorant of the nature and importance of the bagpipe.)

The bagpipe was held in such high regard that Gaelic poets took great offence to and levied strong criticism against those who played the pipes poorly. The poet *Donnchadh Bàn Mac an t-Saoir* castigated one such piper in his poem "*Aoir Uisdein*" (Lampoon on Hugh):

Nan cluinneadh sibh muc a' rùcail
geòidh is tunnagan a' ràcail
'S ann mar sin a bha piob Uisdein
Brònach muladach a' ranaich ...

Should you hear a pig grunting,
Geese cackling or ducks quacking,
'twas even so that Hugh's bagpipe
Was wailing, mournful and depressing ...

So important were pipers to the clan, that Manson notes "the hereditary pipers were second only to the chiefs of the various clans." Their positions within the clans were hereditary, which is not to say that the skills and art of the hereditary piper was not learned, but to make a piper, it took "seven years of his own learning and seven generations before." The MacCrimmons, the hereditary pipers to MacLeod of Dunvegan, were held to be the most accomplished.

Mac Cruimin, by R.R. MacIan

The tradition of the bagpipe has long been thought to have been dealt a blow by the passing of The Act of Proscription of 1746, following the Jacobites' attempts to reinstate the Stuarts to the throne of Britain. The Act explicitly outlawed Highland dress and weapons of war, and under its terms, the pipes were deemed to be "weapons" and subjected anyone who possessed or played them to penalty. There is some dispute, however, as to whether the Act really pertained to the pipes, as it doesn't explicitly mention the instrument, and there is record of only one piper having been punished until it – and then, that perhaps for treason, rather than piping per se.

However, it might have been the implication of official disapproval of the pipes, combined with the sanctions imposed upon Gaelic culture by the Presbyterian church and the dominant English-language culture, and the forced expulsion of Gaels from the Highlands in the age of the Clearances that led to withering of much of Gaelic culture during the 1800s in the *Gàidhealtachd*. However, in accordance with another Gaelic expression – *Thèid dùthchas an aghaidh nan creag* – Heritage goes against the rocks – the tradition continued underground and in the officially sanctioned venues of the military and eventually reemerged to thrive as we know it today.

One last word: Cultures may be compared by looking at what is different and what is the same. The treatment of the bagpipe in Gaelic (Highland) and English-language (Lowland) cultures affords us such an opportunity. How do these two different cultures treat the idea of a supernatural being playing the pipes?

- In the Lowland culture, we can find numerous references to Satan playing the pipes in a witches' sabbath. Accusations of this activity were taken seriously – and literally – and sometimes resulted in the accused being punished, even executed, for witchcraft.
- In the Highlands, in contrast, the supernatural beings playing the pipes were fairies – of a quite different nature than the Satanic spectres in the Lowlands. The fairyfolk were not evil, though they could be mischievious, but just as often, they were regarded as simply another race of humans, descended from the *Tuatha de Dana* – the People of the Goddess Danu – who preceded the Gaels in Ireland and Scotland. Stories abound about humans in the Highlands encountering festivities of fairyfolk. Sometimes the human would play the pipes and sometimes the human would dance to the fairies' playing. It very often happened that while the human experienced a single night having passed, in the "real" world, it was one year, or even 20 years that had gone by. But the primary difference between the Gaelic Highlands and the English-language lowlands was this: No one in the Highlands was ever burned at the stake for witchcraft or for consorting with the fairies.

Language Notes

's e a' ruith air falbh – lit., *and he running away*: Gaelic allows for this
construction, the use of the verbal noun outside of an independent clause
(that is, without the helping verb *bi*), what in English would be expressed
as something like "and he ran away," or "... as he ran away," or "when he
ran away."

Life advice

Deeds not words

Labhraidh a' bheul ach 's e an gnìomhas a dhearbhas.

The mouth will speak, but it's the deed that will prove.

Your actions speak so loudly, I cannot hear what you say.

In the ballad "Tam Lin" from the Scottish borders, the two young lovers Janet and Tam Lin have spoken of their love for one another, but Janet is called upon to prove her love by her deeds when Tam Lin is kidnapped by the Queen of the Fairies. Tam Lin tells her that on Halloween night, he will ride by with the fairy troop, and if she is to save him, she must grip hold of him and not let go, no matter what frightening thing he is turned into by the fairies' evil magic. There are many versions of the ballad; here is part of one where Tam Lin is telling his belove Janet what she must do:

> They'll turn me in your arms, my love
> Into an awful snake
> But hold me fast and fear me not
> For I'm to be your mate
>
> They'll turn me to a bear so grim,
> And then a lion wild,
> But hold me fast, and fear me not,
> For I am the father of your child.
>
> They'll shape me in your arms, lady,
> Into a hot iron at the fire;
> But hold me fast, don't let me go,
> And I'll be your heart's desire.

Janet's deeds prove equal to her word, and she frees Tam Lin from the clutches of the Fairy Queen.

Life-long learning

Chan eil thu tuilleadh 's sean airson ionnsachadh fhathast

You aren't too old to learn yet.

I (your faithful, diligent, dedicated author) am an advocate of life-long learning. It was in my fifties that I undertook to learn the language of our ancestors, well past the age when many people might think I was not only too old to learn but especially that I was past the age when many linguists would say I was too old to acquire a new language -- language learning being reserved for the young, in the minds of many "experts."

And yet, I began a course of study that incorporated self-guided learning, formal school-based instruction, and private tutoring from a native speaker from the Isle of Harris in the Outer Hebrides (Donald Mcdonald, a man who became a dear friend before he was taken away from us, and who, by the way, espoused the philosophy of "every Gaelic speaker a teacher").

The end result – and I mention this only as an encouragement to others – is that over the past years, I have published two books of Gaelic poetry and three books of English poetry illustrated and translated into Gaelic; I have won the gold medal for written poetry at the Royal National Mòd in Scotland; I have earned a certificate of completion from the Atlantic Gaelic Academy; and I have -- most recently -- graduated from the Gaelic college *Sabhal Mòr Ostaig* on the Isle of Skye in "Gaelic and Related Studies"; and in my writing and teaching, I strive to continue advocating for the language of our *dualchas* – our heritage.

Seann chù a dh'ionnsaich cleasan ùra

Old dog who learned new tricks

Good advice, not always followed

Na sir 's na seachainn an t-sabaid.

Neither seek nor shun a fight.

The proverb suggests a balanced approach to conflict, advocating neither aggression nor avoidance. There's a poignant tale in Gaelic oral and written literature that has been told and retold – with some variations – for more than a thousand years. It involves tragedy of the death of *Ciùinlaoch*, the son of the great Gaelic hero *Cù-Chulainn* at the hands of his own father.

The son, *Ciùinlaoch*, does not know his father. He was conceived during an affair the great hero had with the child's mother while the father was training with the woman-warrior *Scàthach* in Scotland (at a kind of graduate school for young warriors). The time came for *Cù-Chulainn* to return to Ireland and take his position amongst the *Fiann*-- the band of warriors protecting their homeland against invasion. Before Cù-Chulainn departed, he told the mother that if their son came looking for him in Ireland, he was forbidden to disclose who he was.

When *Ciùinlaoch*, the son, comes of age, he goes searching for his father; he sails across the sea separating Gaelic Scotland and Gaelic Ireland. He encounters the protectors of Ireland. They ask him to identify himself. Under the taboo of revealing his identity, the young man refuses to reveal himself. The warriors confronting the young man are not seeking a fight. They just have to do their duty and protect the border. They repeatedly ask, and repeatedly are refused, as *Ciùinlaoch* steadfastly adheres to the *geas* – the oath – that has been imposed upon him. He even refuses to identify himself to *Cù-Chulainn*, his father, in spite of repeated entreaties, and *Cù-Chulainn* is forced by his sense of duty to fight his son, and after a long single-combat, he kills the young *Ciùinlaoch*.

A version of the story that dates back to the tenth century concludes with a poignant image of all nature bewailing the death of *Ciùinlaoch* – a name which means "gentle hero." Here translated from ancient Gaelic:

> [Cù-Chulainn's] cry of lament was raised, [Ciùinlaoch's] grave made, and his stone set up, and to the end of three days no calf was let to their cows by the men of Ulster, to commemorate him.

The last part of this might be a little puzzling, but it is explained by the image of all of nature, all nature's creatures, joining in the cries of lamentation for the death of the "gentle hero." (Imagine the calves wailing and bellowing for their mothers' milk.)

Ancient stories do not always show us people behaving in positive ways. Sometimes, they show characters making misguided choices – and the disastrous outcomes that (not surprisingly) follow. It's not possible to always avoid a fight, but the proverb advises us that whenever we can, we should not seek it, counsel followed in part – but tragically, not in full -- by the warriors of this ancient Gaelic legend.

Teach them while they're young

Am fear nach do dh'ionnsaich aig a' ghlùin, chan ionnsaich e ris an uilinn.

The one who didn't learn at the knee, will not learn at the elbow.

To learn "at the knee" refers to when a child is "knee-high," that is very young. The phrase for somebody who is natively fluent in Gaelic is that they acquired the language "on ghlùin" – from the knee.

This observation is not unique to Gaelic culture but is a maxim acknowledged universally, being similar, for instance, to the English-language expressions "A tree must be bent while it's young," or "Between 3 and 13, bend the twig while it's green," a truth that is borne out by innumerable psychological studies of childhood development: It's a sad truth that children stop listening to their parents and begin attaching more importance to lessons learned from their peers around the time of puberty.

In traditional Gaelic culture, this maxim played out quite practically in the bringing up of children.

Fosterage: the custom of housing a boy in the home of a related family, often a more powerful or influential one. The foster son would be regarded as a brother and son of the family. This practice helped foster and develop feelings of familial loyalty and tied families and clans closer together. Ronald Black in his Commentary on John Gregorson Campbell's *The Gaelic Otherworld* remarks that

> fostership was traditionally the strongest of all ties – *comhdhaltais gu ceud, agus càirdeas gu fichead,* 'fostership to a hundred degrees, and blood-relationship to twenty.' (that is, 'foster-relationships scored 100, while blood relationships only scored a 20 – if that makes more sense).

Formal Education: The Statutes of Iona, passed by the Scottish government in 1609, required that Highland chiefs send their heirs to Lowland, English-language schools, among other things. Here we see the maxim being applied in a negative way, for the purpose of the laws was to expunge Gaelic language and culture in the hearts and minds of those young men who would return to the Highlands imbued with "English" values rather than Gaelic.

Apprenticeship: Even from the very earliest times, male children (traditional Gaelic culture was patriarchal and gender-segregated) were often apprenticed out to inculcate in them the knowledge and the culture of the trade or profession they were intended to follow as adults. The great hero *Cù-Chulainn*, for instance, was sent to play with the other boys who were in training to serve as warriors of the *Fèinne*, the protectors of ancient Gaeldom.

Another legendary Gaelic hero, *Fionn MacCumhaill*, was apprenticed as a boy to an old druid. The legend has it that *Fionn* acquired his great wisdom one day when his master had him mind the cooking of the salmon-of-wisdom, but he (the boy) was not to taste any of the cooking fish. In cooking the fish, Fionn turned it over and accidently burned his thumb. Instinctively, the boy stuck his thumb in his mouth to cool off the burn – and so acquired the wisdom contained in it. Unfortunately, nowadays teaching children is not so easy as feeding them a pill-of-education; the story is obviously mythical, although it does contain the truth of the necessity of teaching children when they're young – *on ghlùin.*

Language Notes

Syntax – Although Gaelic typically structures sentences verb-first, here we have an example of a different kind of structure: a noun followed by a relative clause – *the one **who*** ... so the operative independent clause – the "sentence" part – kind of doubles back.

Am fear	nach	do	dh'ionnsaich	aig a' ghlùin	chan	ionnsaich	e	ris an uilinn.
The **man** (one)	who not	Past particle marker	Learn, past tense ("learned")	at the knee	not	will learn	**he**	at the elbow.

An easier-to-follow translation:

The **<u>one</u>** who doesn't learn at the knee, **<u>he</u>** will not learn at the elbow

illustrates how this structure accommodates the verb-first mandate of Gaelic: the first clause (*the one who*) is a dependent clause, a kind of "branch" that modifies the main "trunk" of the sentence (*he will not learn* ...). (Now you know why grammar was never your favorite subject in school!)

Life changes

Chan eil carraig ann nach caochail sruth.

xx

There isn't a rock that does not change the stream.

Language Notes:

Every obstacle or *carraig* – rock – that we encounter changes the course, or the *sruth* – the current or stream -- of our lives. After encountering such a "rock," we don't get "back on course" – the new course we are on *is* our course, whether we had intended it to be so, or not. (This idea is sometimes referred to as the "butterfly effect," which is so named after the idea that the fluttering of the wings of a butterfly in the Amazon -- the forest, not the online retailer -- can effect a hurricane across the world.)

Americans should be aware how the refusal of Rosa Parks to give up her bus seat in segregated Alabama triggered the Civil Rights movement of the 1960s.

A three-legged stool is a small thing, and such was the "stone" that ignited the religious War of Three Nations in 17th century Britain. A Scottish woman, Jenny Geddes, objected to the preaching of a liturgy that supported the establishment of the King as head of the Scottish church (the Scottish Christians, strongly supporting the separation of Church and State, opposed the government meddling in their religion). She stood up in church at threw her stool at the preacher's head, which act set off riots in Scotland's capital city, and subsequently the revolution that saw the overturning of the nation's entire order and system of governance.

Diverting the stream of history: One might not think that the width of a small bridge could affect the course of history, yet it was just the narrowness of Stirling Bridge that allowed Sir William Wallace to trap a large portion of the attacking English army in a bottleneck – forcing the invaders into the water of the river to be slaughtered and drowned – and thus gain a crucial victory in the Scottish War of Independence.

And talk about an actual stone: The Stone of Destiny -- *Clach-Chrùnaidh na h-Alba* – the stone on which Scottish kings were traditionally crowned -- has long been symbolic of Scottish nationhood. Its theft by the English King Edward I in 1296 and its rescue and return by a band of Scottish college students on Christmas Day 1950 were regarded as vastly important symbolic events in the history of the Scottish nation.

Talking sense to a fool

Is duilich ciall a thoirt do amadan.

It's hard to talk sense to a fool.

One of the most tragic examples of the truth of this proverb is in the events that led up to the battle on Drummossie Moor, known as the Battle of Culloden Moor – a battle between the Highland army of Prince Charles, claimant to the throne of Great Britain, and the British army of the Hanoverian King George II. The Highland army was exhausted after several days of retreat from England, and even more so after a failed night-march during which they tried unsuccessfully to find and attack the government troops, only to return to their camp, exhausted and hungry.

An Incident in the Rebellion of 1745, by David Morier

The advisors of the Prince urged him to retreat and regroup – that the condition of his warriors and of the field were not favorable for victory. But Prince Charles persisted – there was no talking sense to him, as the proverb puts it. As one of the Highland Chiefs said later, "None but a mad fool would have fought that day" (as reported by John Prebble in his book *Culloden*). The refusal of the Prince – the Bonnie Prince Charlie of history and legend – to heed the counsel of his generals spelled doom for the Gaelic army, and the destruction of the ancient Gaelic ways in the Highlands of Scotland. Even today, nearly 300 years after that fateful day, I have heard Gaels refer to that turning-point event as BC and AC – *Before Culloden* and *After Culloden*. And all because the fool of the Prince would not listen to sense.

Language Notes

Is duilich – The assertive verb (*Is*) can introduce an adjective rather than a noun. This is done for emphasis of the adjective, literally *Is difficult* (rather than *tha e duilich – it is difficult*).

duilich – Although often translated as "sorry" as in *Tha mi duilich sin a chluinntin* – I'm sorry to here that – duilich can also mean "difficult" or "hard." We're reminded that no two languages map 1-for-1 on each other. While there may be exact matches, especially in terms of borrowed terms for technology – for instance, *càr* in Gaelic maps pretty closely, if not exactly, onto *car* in English – it's not uncommon that the meaning of words overlap, rather than match exactly.

Gain and loss

Cha dèanar buannachd gun chall

Gain is not made without loss

Roughly equivalent to *no pain, no gain*, but a little bit different. The English expression prescribes the *pain* as being a necessary precursor to the *gain*. In other words, in the context in which it is often applied in contemporary culture, if you want to experience the gain of fitness or weight loss, you have to go through the pain of working out. The Gaelic framing is a little different, for it expresses the idea of what economists call *opportunity cost*: You cannot gain something without a corresponding giving up of something else.

For example, over the centuries, English has replaced Gaelic as the dominant language in Scotland, precipitously since the advent of the 20th century. The spread of English was often seen by Gaels themselves as a gain in terms of economic opportunity and integration into the larger, more affluent, and more powerful British nation. However, this gain was offset by the loss of Gaelic as a primary language and the erosion of our cultural heritage.

Language Notes

cha dèanar – the future or habitual passive form of the verb, in the negative, as in this will not be done, or this is not (usually) done.

Okay, but, what does that mean, and what's going on with this? To explain, we might need a little grammar refresher: The *passive voice* is the form in which something is done to something else, rather than somebody or something doing the action, as in *the ball was hit by the boy*, or in the case of the future, *the ball will be hit by the boy*, rather than the more common (in English, anyway) *the boy hit the ball*, or *the boy will hit the ball*.

Furthermore, in Gaelic, the future tense can serve either as expressing the literal future, or a *habitual or continual action or state of being*. You can see the contrast with English which expresses this "eternal" state by the use of the present tense – *gain **is** not made*, vs. the Gaelic – *gain **will** not **be made**.*

In Gaelic, one way to express the passive voice is the direct and economical inflection of the verb as a "true" passive future tense, which takes the form of the *root verb + (e)ar*, lenited if it's a positive statement, unlenited if it's negative or a question, so in this case

- dhèanar = will be done
- cha dèanar = will not be done
- an dèanar = will x be done?

And, aren't you sorry you asked!

Desperate times

Feumaidh am fear a bhios an èiginn beart èiginneach a dhèanamh.

The man who is in desperation has to do desperate deeds.

Scots are no strangers to desperate times, and the innovative stratagems they've used to overcome their difficulties are numerous. Just a couple:

Apocryphally, ingenious Scots in the town of Dundee made use of a shipload of stranded, rotting Seville oranges. The spoilage of the shipment threatened a tremendous loss to the shipowners and businessmen who'd invested in the cargo. according to legend, the Scots of Dundee landed upon the scheme to make marmalade out of the fermenting oranges and thereby started the now famous Dundee marmalade enterprise. (Sort of the Scottish equivalent of *if all you have are lemons* ... only, in this case, *if all you have are rotting oranges...*)

Not all desperate measures are successful. The measures are desperate because they are against long odds. The measures are rare because the odds of their success are low. For instance, before the fateful battle of Culloden, the Jacobite Highland troops of Prince Charles attempted a march in pitch black, fog-socked night landscape in an attempt to take the government troops by surprise.

Unfortunately, the night march wasn't successful; the night was dark, the Highlanders lost their way and never found their target, the enemy army, and had to return to their camp exhausted, hungry, and depleted, which condition contributed to their defeat the next day.

Language Notes

Syntax: A lot of stuff going on here. Let's take a look. First, a reminder,

Feumaidh am fear a bhios an èiginn beart èiginneach a dhèanamh

In English, the sentence would read something like "The man who is in need must do a desperate deed," but in Gaelic, the "must" and the "do" are separated by nearly every other word in the sentence, partly because the "must" is the operative or helping verb of the sentence, and as we know, must come first, followed by the subject ("the man") and then before we get to the final verb ("do"), we have to front the object – that is, slip the object in before the "do." Perhaps, the following chart will make this clearer:

Feumaidh	am fear	a bhios	an èiginn	beart èiginneach	**a dhèanamh**
Must	the man / the one	who is	in distress / necessity	desperate deed (or, lit. *deed desperate*)	**do**

Minor notes:

an èiginn – a contraction for ***ann an èiginn*** ("in distress")

a bhios – the future independent relative form of the verb *bi* ("be" in English). In English, we would say "the man **will be**" and "the man **who will be**" (note the verb retains its form regardless of being part of an independent clause, or a dependent relative clause). Not so in Gaelic, in which we would say, ***Bidh** am fear* ("the man will be") and *Am fear **a bhios*** (The man who will be).

Our beloved language never ceases to delight and surprise!

Go with what you've got

An ràmh as fhaisge air làimh, iomair leis.

The oar that is closest at hand, row with *it*.

Use what you've got, don't neglect to do something for lack of what you wished you had. Another way of phrasing this might be, don't let the perfect (or your idea of the perfect) be the enemy of the good.

In the Western Highlands, very often the farmland was sparce, if not totally barren. In such a desolate landscape, the people gathered seaweed from the shore and carried inland where they spread the *feamainn* intermixing it with soil into planting areas surrounded by low stone walls. James Hunter in his *book The Making of the Crofting Community* quotes one observer as writing, some [lazybeds] are no bigger than a dining table, and possibly the same height from the rock, carefully built up with turfs arried there in creels by the women and girls. One of thee lazybeds will yield a sheaf of oats or a bucket of potatoes.

However, these expedients could not support an entire population beyond starvation levels, and for that reason, many Highland Gaels were forced to emigrate.

Language Notes

as fhaisge = that is the closest -- the comparative of ***faisg*** (near; *faisg **air*** = near **to**)

Iomair leis = row with it; *leis* = the prepositional pronoun for *with him/it, ràmh* being masc. and therefore a 'him'

syntax: Rather than a structure that English-speakers might think was more straight-forward -- *Row with the oar that's nearest at hand* -- the sentence calls our attention to the **oar** first – emphasizing that -- and then circles back around to what we're to do with it.

Clean your own house

Sguab do theallach fhèin mus tèid thu a sguabadh teallach duine eile

**Scrub your own hearth before you go scrubbing the
hearth of somebody else.**

Similar to the maxim that "People in glasshouses shouldn't throw stones," or the Biblical admonition of "Let him who is without sin throw the first stone," but different in that the Gaelic proverb refers to *doing*, rather than just speaking. In other words, it's not about criticizing (or **not**) but rather about taking care of your own business, correcting your own deficiencies, before you launch into correcting other people's.

Language Notes

teallach -- fireside, hearth, fireplace, sort of the equivalent of today's modern kitchen.

Interior of a Highland Cottage by John Glass.

Careful with the beards of strangers!

Na spìon fiosaig fir nach aithne dhut

Do not pluck the bear of a stranger.

In a confrontation with someone you don't know, be careful because you don't know what you're getting into. Good advice in the age of road rage!

Language Notes

Na – *na* has a number of homophones (words that are spelled the same but have different meanings). Here the word forms the negative of the command, as in don't (or **do not**) pluck. However, it should be understood that unlike in English where the negative command contains a verb – albeit a helping verb (do), the **na** in Gaelic contains no such verb content, but is entirely a negative, like a **not** (as in ***not*** *pluck the beard* ... etc).

Keeping secrets

Chan e sgeul-rùin a th' ann nam biodh fios aig triuir air.

It is no secret when three know it.

Wise advice not to be a blabbermouth – and this means, not telling your secret to anyone!

I often wonder at people who post pictures and videos of themselves doing the most shameful deeds -- even committing crimes -- on the Internet: The teacher whose profession demands she maintain an aura of respectibility posting pictures of herself behaving like a drunken teenager on spring break, and then is surprised when the religious girl's school we works for fires her. Employees who bad-mouth their bosses on social media. The bank robber who posted a video of him flashing the cash he had just stolen on Youtube.

It's not a secret when three know it – and certainly not when millions know it. If you want to keep something secret, keep it to yourself!

Language Notes

Sgeul-rùin – secret, literally a *secret story (sgeul* = story; *rùn* = secret; but also, *rùn* can mean "desire" or "love")

Nam ... **biodh** – Gaelic has a few words for "if." This is one of the words for "if" in the conditional, counter-factual sense. It uses the conditional form of the verb (here, *biodh*). We can see a parallel usage in English: As my mother used to say to me,

- "If I **had** a million dollars, I'd give it all to you." (she didn't, and there was no chance she would have that amount of money, but I appreciated the thought)
- If I **have** the money, I'll take us all out to the movies. Let me check my purse. (There was a chance we might go out! Yay!)

The hero's quest

Strength vs. cunning

Thèid seòltachd thar spionnadh.

Cunning beats strength.

In Gaelic folk literature, it's not always the case that the hero is strong and fearless. More often than not, the hero – who may be either a man or a woman, a boy or a girl – achieves success through cunning, as this saying goes.

Many proverbs reflect a broader context – history, experience, story, fable – and sometimes that context is lost to us, leaving us only with the observation, so all we have remaining is the proverb itself. However, in this case, we do have the story of a donkey who is threatened with being eaten by a lion. The donkey saves himself by tricking the lion into thinking that he – the donkey – is mightier and more ferocious than the King of Beasts. Hence the aphorism, cunning is more powerful than strength – an important truth to remember if you are a member of a small, relatively weak society surrounded by much larger and more powerful forces.

Kindness as a heroic quality

An làmh a bheir, 's i a gheibh.

The hand that gives is the hand that gathers.

A *bannock* is a bread of uneven shape, cooked on a stone or gridle, sometimes with ingredients – savouries First, or fruits -- baked in.

A story attached to this proverb tells of sisters "going out into the world to seek their fortune" – one is greedy and takes all that she can from her impoverished mother – the big bannock -- along with a curse, and her greed and selfishness result in the failure of her quest because she is selfish and greedy with all whom she meets. While the other sister, who is generous, open-hearted, and sharing, takes the small bannock, leaving the mother with enough to feed herself; this daughter finds success because she is open and caring with all whom she meets – both human and animal – and they are the same with her and help her in the furtherance of her quest.

As so many of these proverbs come connected to stories or situations that might or might not be in the written record, so does this one.

There's a story of poor mother with two daughters. The older one told her mother that she was ready to go out into the world for herself.

The mother offered her a little piece of a bannock with her blessing, or a large piece and her curse. The girl opted for the large piece, even knowing the mother was hard put to feed herself and the other children.

Is fheàrr am bonnach beag leis a' bheannachd, na 'm bonnach mòr leis a' mhollachd.

Better the little bannock with a blessing than a large bannock with a curse

In the course of the story, the girl likewise refuses to share or help others. She subsequently fails in her quest and is put under a spell by an evil witch.

When the younger daughter goes to the mother with the same wish – to go out on her own, the mother makes the same offer – the little piece with a blessing or the big piece with a curse. This daughter, being of a generous and sharing nature, chooses the smaller piece and the mother's blessing. The girl likewise shares with those she encounters, including small hungry animals who ask for a bit to eat. When the girl encounters the witch, the animals she was kind to come to her aid. She defeats the witch, frees her selfish sister, and returns home with a treasure to help her mother and her other siblings.

All of which underlines the Gaelic culture values of generosity and connectivity.

Surviving by your wits

"Mas e duine a tha an seo, 's aotrom a tha e!" thuirt an t-each-uisge.

"If it's a human that is here, it's light!" the water-horse said (shaking the skirt of the girl he wanted to kidnap).

Something quite common in Gaelic tales is the resourcefulness and bravery of girls and women. The Gaelic heroine does not wait for the knight in shining armor, or any other type of rescuing hero to come save her.

More often than not, as she lacks the strength to direct combat that which threatens her – she survices by her wits.

There's the story of the girl who is about to be kidnapped by *an t-each-uisge* – the "water horse," a fearsome monster who lives beneath the thwaters of the loch and feeds on unwary young people. She escapes by throwing her plaid over a nearby heather, which deceives the monster long enough to allow her to escape:

Language Notes

The assertive verb – *is* – is most often used to assert that one thing is another thing, as in even simple statements like

- Is mise Mìcheal – I am Michael

but is sometimes used for emphasis, for example, to introduce an adjective, as in:

- **Is** toilichte a tha an nighean. Is happy that is the girl.
- **Is** minig a tha e a' dol dhan taigh-seinnse. Is often that he goes to the pub.

The fate of heroes

Chan eil gaisgeach mòr ann a tha do-leònadh.

There is not a great hero who is invulnerable.

Unlike in American mythology, there is no Superman in Gaelic culture, no hero who is invulnerable and almighty, but only mortals who through their efforts and their determination face the risks inherent in their service. An entire treatise could be written on the topic of the vulnerbility of heroes. Unlike a recent politician who was known to disparage soldiers fallen in battle or taken prisoner ("I like people who weren't captured"), in Gaelic culture heroes are heroic because of the risks they take on behalf of the community – the clan or the nation – and it is well known that those risks entail the very real likelihood of eventual defeat and death.

A hero is not a hero because he is invulnerable, but rather just the opposite – he is a hero because he is vulnerable, and in a word, mortal, subject to defeat and death. He is a hero because in a sense, he defies that fate, challenges it, even welcomes it in his service to the good of the community (as he conceives of it). . The arc of the legend of Cuchullain, one of the greatest heroes in Gaelic mythology, illustrates this. His life-story moves from his youth as a precocious youthful warrior to a hero who has himself strapped to a standing stone in his battle against the invaders of his homeland so that he would die on his feet, facing the enemy, protecting his *duthaich* to the last.

Language Notes:

Gaisgeach = hero. Learn this word! Very important in Gaelic!

Do-leònadh – called attention to it here because of the "do-" prefix, which serves somewhat like *un-* or *in-* or *non-* in English. *Leòn* relates to "wound," so *do-leònadh* would be "not wounded," or "unwounded."

Goals

Bidh an t-ubhal as fheàrr air a mheangan as àirde.

The best apple is on the highest branch.

While people in Gaelic culture have many times in our history been constrained and contained within narrow circumstances by either natural forces or the force of other nations, and because of these restraints the culture possesses a healthy practical aspect to it, there is no shortage of lofty goals which Gaels have aspired to.

The dream of a united, independent Scotland has inspired Gael and Gall – Highlander and Lowlander – alike for more than a thousand years. Sometimes, we have achieved it, and sometimes we have lost our grip on it, or even lost sight of it, but we have always come back to it – from the Wars of Independence under Sir William Wallace and King Robert the Bruce; to the fight to restore Gaelic self-sufficiency under Bonnie Prince Charlie; to the struggle for that high "apple" of freedom and independence today under the leadership of the Scottish National Party.

In the late 19th and early 20th century, Gaels mounted a movement to revive and preserve Gaelic language, culture, and literature that was known as the Gaelic Renaissance. Prominent literary figures such as Sorley MacLean and Hugh MacDiarmid were leaders of this attempt to stem the tide of centuries of decline and suppression. The high "apple" of restoring a flourishing Gaelic culture, free from oppression and marginalization, inspired many Gaels and continues to do so today.

The Gaelic code of honor that places bravery, honesty, generosity, and loyalty above all other values and that animates and informs many of the proverbs in this book is another such "high apple."

Principal Sources

Bauer, Micheal & Uilleam MacDhonnchaidh. *Am Faclair Beag - A New English / Scottish Gaelic Dictionary Incorporating Dwelly and Faclair nan Gnàthasan-cainnte by Cairnwater Consulting and Akerbeltz.* https://www.faclair.com/

Bennett, Margaret. *Scottish Customs: From the Cradle to the Grave.* 2004.

Burns, Robert. *Collected Poems.*

Bruford, Alan J. & Macdonald, Donald A. *Scottish Traditional Tales.* 2018.

Campbell, J.F. Popular Tales of the West Highlands. (v's I & II). 1860.

Campbell, J.F. *Leabhar na Fèinne: Vol. I. Gaelic Texts. Heroic Gaelic Ballads.* 1872.

Campbell, J.F. *More West Highland Tales. v. I & II.* 1960 & 1994.

Campbell, John Gregorson. *The Gaelic Otherworld: Superstitions of the Highlands and Islands of Scotland and Witchcraft and Second Sight in the Highlands and Islands.* ed., Ronald Black. 2005. (Original edition 1900.)

Campbell, Thomas. *Poems of Thomas Campbell.* 1904.

Carmicheal, Alexander. *Carmina Gadelica. Ortha nan Gaidheal.* 1900.

Dwelly, Edward. *The Illustrated Gaelic Dictionary.* 1918.

Hunter, James. *The Making of the Crofting Community.* 2010.

Mackintosh's Collection of Gaelic Proverbs Familiar Phrases. 1819.

Mac an t-Saoir, Donnchadh Bàn. *Òrain Dhonnchaidh Bhàin.* (The Songs of Duncan Ban Macintyre). ed., Angus MacLeod. 1952.

MacDonald, T.D. *Gaelic Proverbs and Proverbial Sayings.* 1926.

MacGill-Eain, Somhairle. *O Choille gu Bearraidh: Dàin Chruinnichte.* (From Wood to Ridge: Collected Poems). 1989.

MacGilleMhàrtainn, Màrtainn (Martin Martin). *A Description of the Western Islands of Scotland.* 1716.

M'Gregor, J. *The Dean of Lismore's Book. A Selection of Ancient Gaelic Poetry.* From a Manuscript Collection made by Sir James M'Gregor, Dean of

Lismore, in the beginning of the Sixteenth Century. c. 1512. Thomas M'Lauchlan, trans edit; Skene, William, notes, edit. Reprinted, 1862.

MacIan, R. R. *The Clans of the Scottish Highlands.* 1845.

Manson, W.L. *The Highland Bagpipe: Its History, literature, and music, with some account of the traditions, superstitions, and anecdotes relating to the instrument and its tunes.* 1901.

Mark, Colin. *The Gaelic English Dictionary.* 2003.

Meyer, Kuno. "The Death of Conla." *Ériu.* 1904.

Newton, Michael. "'Woe to him who has lost his voice': Re-discovering the Gaelic literature of the Lennox and Menteith," in *Literary Tourism, the Trossachs and Walter Scott*, edited by Ian Brown, 98-112. Glasgow: Association for Scottish Literary Studies, 2012.

Nicolson, Alexander. *A collection of Gaelic Proverbs and Familiar Sayings.* 1882.

Ó Giollagan, Conchúr; Gòrdan Camshron, Pàdruig Moireach, Brian Ó Curnáin, Iain Caimbeul, Brian MacDonald, & Tamás Péterváry. *The Gaelic Crisis in the Vernacular Community: A comprehensive sociolinguistic survey of Scottish Gaelic.* 2020.

Prebble, John. *Culloden.* 1961.

Prebble, John. *The Darien Disaster: A Scots Colony in the New World.* 1969.

Prebble, John. *The Highland Clearances.* 1969.

Richards, Eric. *The Highland Clearances.* 2013.

Scott, Ronald McNair. *Robert the Bruce, King of Scots.* 1996.

Scott, Walter. *The Fair Maid of Perth.* 1828.

Scott, Walter. *The Heart of the Midlothian.* 1818.

Stevenson, Robert Louis. *Kidnapped.* 1886.

Watts, Elidh. *Gun Fhois: Sgeulachdan mun Dà Shealladh.* 1987.